D1613040

Rural Industrialization

RURAL INDUSTRIALIZATION

The Impact of Industrialization on
Two Rural Communities in Western Ireland

DENIS I. F. LUCEY

and

DONALD R. KALDOR

GEOFFREY CHAPMAN
LONDON DUBLIN MELBOURNE 1969

Geoffrey Chapman Ltd
18 High Street, Wimbledon, London SW 19

Geoffrey Chapman (Ireland) Ltd
5–7 Main Street, Blackrock, County Dublin

Geoffrey Chapman Pty Ltd
44 La Trobe Street, Melbourne, Vic 3000, Australia

First published 1969

This book is set in 11 on 13pt Baskerville

Printed in Great Britain by A. Wheaton & Co., Exeter, Devon

Contents

5

Acknowledgements

Financial support for this study was provided in large part by the Agricultural Development Council, New York, the Central Statistics Office, Dublin, and the Economic and Social Research Institute, Dublin. The authors also wish to acknowledge the helpful assistance and contributions of Dr M. D. McCarthy, Dr R. C. Geary, Professor R. O'Connor, Rev. Professor J. Kavanagh, Rev. Dr C. K. Ward and Dr L. P. F. Smith in Ireland. In Iowa, Professors E. O. Heady, E. A. Brady, W. A. Fuller, N. V. Strand and H. Baker made many helpful suggestions both on the economic and statistical aspects of the study. Facilities and finance were also provided by the Iowa Agricultural Experiment Station and by Iowa State University.

The study would not have been possible without the splendid cooperation of the management personnel at the plants in Tubbercurry and in Scarriff, who provided every facility requested by the authors. Neither would the study have been possible without the good will of the many respondents, both within the factories and throughout the rest of the study areas, who took time and pains to answer the questions asked them and provided much of the needed information. The authors are deeply grateful for this cooperation.

Foreword

What actually happens when as a result of a successful industrial
development policy a new plant appears in a hitherto farming
community? There are many angles from which this question can
be answered. One can inquire for example into the economic
success of the firm itself, into the changes in the community's
values and power structure, or into what happens if through some
misfortune the process is put into reverse and the new plant has
to contract or close down. In this study Denis Lucey and Donald
Kaldor consider the impact of new plants in two communities in
the west of Ireland on jobs, emigration, income, spending patterns,
and these communities' hitherto dominant occupation of farming.

The most striking conclusion is about the impact on farming.
For intelligent and relatively well-educated young farmers with
too little land industrial employment has proved to be the way
out, in the sense not only of providing a new source of work and
income but of enabling them to farm more effectively and increase
their farm output. When the farm operator takes an industrial
job the input of labour into his farm falls. It does not, however,
fall by the full amount of his own day's work, for he still puts in
a substantial amount of time on his farm, and his wife and family
contribute to the farm work more than they otherwise would.
Because there is no longer surplus labour available, farm work
tends to be thought out more carefully, so that the labour
available goes further. Industrial earnings tend to be ploughed
back into farm equipment and facilities. Farmers working in
industry report that they are using more fertilizer, have bought
extra cattle, are hiring more plant from outside, and generally
that their farms are better managed. Patterns of farming change
to fit the greater availability of money and smaller availability of

labour. In these two communities there has been a switch from more labour-intensive activities such as crops and dairying to dry cattle. All these factors together show that at least in the short run industrialization in these communities has meant not a switch from agricultural to industrial output, but an increase in both together. The qualification about the short run is necessary, for a longer run of experience would be needed to show, for example, whether long-range measures of land conservation such as drainage will be as well looked after under part-time farming as under full-time, or whether working at two jobs at once will always remain satisfying to farm operators themselves.

Another interesting finding is about the size of the difference in earnings which potential emigrants from rural communities like these are prepared to accept if a job is available in their own community. At the time of the survey men in the new plant were averaging £11–£12 a week. They estimated the alternative earnings available to them if the plant had not been there at an average of £2–£6 a week according to category, supposing always that some kind of local job had been available. Their expected alternative earnings if they had migrated to Britain or elsewhere in Ireland, on the other hand, averaged £18–£20. The survey shows that the establishment of the new plant not only reduced substantially the amount of emigration which would otherwise have taken place but had some—though limited—effect in inducing former emigrants to return home.

Other findings of the survey are in expected directions but none the less encouraging for that. Household expenditure and standards of living increased. Local shopkeepers got the lion's share of the increased spending, though the major regional shopping centre for each community gained substantially as well. Recruitment was from a fairly wide area within roughly a twelve-mile radius of the plants. The recruiting pull was, however, strongest in the communities nearest to the plants, and in these growth centres there was a tendency for people to move in and for population to increase both for this reason and through the stoppage or reversal of emigration.

The whole picture given by the survey is most encouraging. Aspects of rural industrialization not covered by this survey such as those mentioned above must of course not be forgotten. Studies of Irish experience with respect to a number of them have recently been completed or are under way. Dr Damien Hannan, for example, has completed a study of the motives which lead potential emigrants from an Irish county to accept or reject local opportunities, or to pick up or reject social obligations such as are often felt by the members of farm families. There has been an official survey of the success of grant-aided industries in Ireland. Ireland is gradually becoming equipped with the means for a realistic assessment of the effects of its own drive for development, and Lucey and Kaldor's study is a substantial contribution to this. It carries also a wider lesson for those concerned with rural industrialization anywhere in the world.

> Michael P. Fogarty
> Director
> The Economic and Social Research Institute
> Dublin

3 April 1969

I

Introduction

The development problem of a less developed area is normally regarded as that of converting a "traditional" society which is largely dependent on subsistence or near-subsistence agriculture, though possibly combined with the export of a few primary commodities, but providing a low level of income per capita, into a "modern" society in which secular growth of income per capita is incorporated in the economic and social system through the development of automatic mechanisms fostering capital accumulation, technological advance and sustained increases in the skill of the labour force.

Even a cursory examination of the economies of what are conventionally referred to as the "developed" countries suggests that one of the more noticeable features of development is the abundance of manufacturing industry from which the wealth of the developed countries would appear to spring. As a result of this, in the view of those having concern for the advancement of the less developed areas, to quote Mountjoy (31, p. 66),[1] "it is not surprising that the introduction of manufacturing industry should be regarded uncritically as a panacea".

Less developed countries thus tend to favour policies of "industrialization" in order to further such objectives as the provision of employment for growing populations (or even for already under-employed populations), the raising of income per capita and thus presumably of standards of living, the improvement of

[1] Numerals in parentheses refer to the list of works cited below, pp 199–201.

a balance of payments situation or even the desire for national prestige which an industrial economy might provide in relation to other producers of primary products. However, even in the developed countries there is also considerable interest in the promotion of industrial development in rural areas.

Most of these areas within the developed countries have in the relatively recent past been characterized by declining employment opportunities frequently accompanied by net emigration of population. In comparison with other areas within the same country, these areas would be ones having relatively low levels of income per capita. Furthermore, these areas have scarcely any manufacturing activity. Recourse has frequently been had to the fostering of manufacturing activity in such areas as a means of maintaining or even expanding the economic base of those areas.

Hence, the implementation of policies to promote manufacturing activities has been of interest, not only to the governments of the less developed nations, but also to the governments of the more developed nations because of the existence of relatively less developed areas within their own countries.

The establishment of a new manufacturing plant in a community may be expected to have both economic and social effects on that community. One may expect that the incidence and magnitude of these effects will vary with the type and size of the new manufacturing plant and also with certain characteristics of the community involved. One of the more apparent effects to be expected would be an increase in the availability of employment opportunities.

Frequently, the establishment of such manufacturing plants in economically depressed areas is encouraged in the hope that they will play an important part in the process of providing off-farm employment opportunities locally for those who might otherwise be obliged to leave those areas in search of employment. This is considered as a policy alternative to the movement of labour from those areas to the relatively more industrialized areas within the country.

The study focuses on the impact of recently established manufacturing plants on two predominantly rural communities in Western Ireland. More specifically, the objectives are:

(a) to determine the relative amount of transfer of agricultural manpower to industry;

(b) to determine the direct effects of industrialization on employment, population, income and household expenditure;

(c) to determine the direct effect of industrialization on agricultural resource efficiency, farm organization, farm investment and the level and mix of farm output;

(d) to estimate the spatial incidence of the direct effects of industrialization;

(e) to determine the nature of any selectivity forces operating to affect the incidence and magnitude of the direct effects.

Knowledge of the specific effects of industrial development in Irish rural communities should be of interest to residents of those communities. In addition it should be of interest to residents or groups in other areas in Ireland who are interested in community development. Furthermore, this knowledge should be of interest to local governmental and central governmental agencies, providing them with some measure of the effectiveness of programs and policies designed to foster industrial development in such areas.

However, a wider base of interest is also claimed for this study. This arises from the comparative analysis of the effects of industrial development on rural communities at different levels of income per capita. Many resources, both in terms of professional manpower and other physical and monetary resources, are currently being devoted by the governments of the developed countries and by international organizations to the problem of aiding the developmental processes of the very underdeveloped countries. Lacking specific information on the degree to which the introduction of various policies, programs or institutions will affect these countries, the organizations responsible have frequently had to rely almost exclusively on their knowledge of the impact which such policies and so on have had in countries like the United States or the more developed Western European nations as a guide to formulating developmental programs for these underdeveloped countries.

In a recent evaluation of the successes and failures of developmental policies aimed at the modernization of subsistence agriculture, Wharton has stated (39, p. 266):

> The real downfall in agricultural development programs to date has been the failure to recognize that agricultural development must be analyzed in its complex totality, focusing on the key interacting facets, each of which must be studied in a particular context and in a continuing ongoing fashion. . . . Moreover, the critical problems in any one country or region need not be the same as in another. Even where a program attacks successfully a combination of critical factors, we must recognize that there is a very little transferability to another problem situation.

Ireland, especially Western Ireland, lies at an intermediate level of development. If it can be demonstrated that, for any specific policy or program, the effect of its introduction in advanced countries like the United States and in intermediate countries like Ireland has been roughly similar, then a much stronger case can be made for an a priori expectation that such a policy would have a success potential in the less developed countries greater than the success potential of a policy which had produced widely differing results following its introduction in the advanced countries and in intermediate countries such as Ireland.

It is with the modest hope of contributing some information on both these facets of concern that the present study was undertaken.[2]

---

[2] Related research has been conducted on industrial development in Eastern Iowa by one of the authors. Studies of rural industrialization have also been made in Indiana, Louisiana, Mississippi, Ohio, Utah, West Virginia, etc. In Europe, there has been related research in Scandinavia and the E.E.C. countries. The authors plan to present detailed comparative analyses of these studies, especially the Irish and Eastern Iowa studies, in a later publication.

Industrialization and Economic Development

Problems of growth and development are matters of critical concern to economists and other social scientists of the current era. The critical nature of these problems is obvious in the case of the many relatively underdeveloped countries which have achieved independence since World War II.

Problems of growth are likewise important to the developed countries both in terms of their own economies and also in relation to their programs of assistance to the less developed countries. This widespread concern has been further evidenced by the designation of the nineteen sixties as "United Nations Development Decade" by the United Nations Organisation (4, p. 1).

Economic growth of a country or an area may be defined as an upward secular trend in its real income. Many writers use the terms economic growth and economic development interchangeably. However, strictly speaking, economic development refers to the process by which an economy passes from a "traditional" to a "modern" stage, whereas economic growth can occur within each of these stages and during the transition. A further source of confusion in the literature is the apparent lack of distinction between economic growth and economic progress which may be defined as an upward secular trend in real income per capita. Thus, depending on the direction and magnitude of changes in its population, an area may experience various combinations of growth and progress over any given interval of time.

Rudiments of a theory of economic growth are evident in the writings of the Mercantilists who flourished in the seventeenth century and regarded the non-agricultural sector as the source of growth. The French physiocrats in the eighteenth century were also concerned with growth, but assigned the critical role to agriculture.

Many economists from the late eighteenth to the late nineteenth century added copiously to the literature concerning growth, its sources and implications. Among the more notable were the contributions of Adam Smith, David Ricardo and Karl Marx.

In the late nineteenth century rapid economic growth occurred in Western Europe and the United States. The interest of economists in the factors affecting growth subsided, to be replaced by the development of theories of resource allocation and pricing, which occupied the forefront of economic thought from that time until the nineteen thirties.

In the aftermath of the great depression of the nineteen thirties most economists, following Keynes (27), focused on the problem of maintaining full employment and the aggregate real demand for goods and services. Interest in the allocation problem thus waned while, in the wake of the economic boom following World War II, interest in the stagnation theory declined also. There was a resurgence of concern with problems of economic growth, both in the developed countries and also in the newly emerging nations.

The immediate post-Keynesian growth theories were of a unisectoral nature, notably those of Harrod (8) and Domar (3). These general theories tended to stress the importance of a sub-stained increase in capital accumulation so that an economy might realize its growth potential in terms of income. Attention was then focused on the capital-labour and capital-output ratios.

The emergence of a serious study of the economics of under-development *per se* began to occur in the nineteen forties, with the consideration of problems of economies characterized by economic dualism, that is, economies having a large "traditional" sector (usually assumed to have a significant amount of "disguised unemployment") existing alongside but practically economically independent of a small "modern" sector. Rosenstein-Rodan (35, p. 202) asserted in 1943 that there existed an "agrarian excess population" in East and South-East Europe amounting to 20–25 million people out of the total population of 100–110 million. "If the principles of international division of labour are to be applied," he wrote, "labour must either be transported towards capital (emigration), or capital must be transported towards labour (industrialization)."

Rosenstein-Rodan felt that emigration and resettlement would, however, present so many difficulties in immigration areas (and in emigration areas) that it could not be considered feasible on a large scale and hence "a very considerable part of the task will have to be solved by industrialization" (35, p. 202).

Mandelbaum in a 1945 monograph presented a detailed model of an industrialization process in South-East Europe. In recommending industrialization as a policy measure for that area Mandelbaum stated that "the economic case for industrialization of densely populated backward countries rests upon this mass phenomenon of disguised rural unemployment" (30, p. 2).

Since then, many economists, e.g. Leibenstein (28) and Hirschman (12), have argued so strongly that the opportunities for economic growth in all countries are to be found primarily in the expansion of non-farm industries that Schultz (36, p. 133) has recently coined the phrase "industrial fundamentalism" to describe some of the more extreme views.

Other economists, e.g. Nicholls (33) and Heady (9), have drawn attention to the situations where agriculture can have an advantage over durable and producer goods industries in a development program by giving a pay-off in the near term.

Most economists have tended to favour a balanced approach, recognizing that effective industrial development of the less developed countries cannot proceed effectively without corresponding appropriate development of agriculture. Lewis (29, p. 124), for instance, has argued that "an agricultural and an industrial revolution always go together, the first releasing the labour which the second draws off the land".

Rigorous models of the development of a dual economy have been presented by Jorgensen (25) and by Fei and Ranis (5). The latter model is one of the more elaborate in the field of economic development. Speaking of "the typical labour surplus type of underdeveloped economy", the authors state (5, p. 7):

> In such a dualistic (two-sector) setting the heart of the development problem may be said to lie in the gradual shifting of the center of gravity of the economy from the agricultural to the industrial sector. Such a process can be gauged in terms of the re-allocation of the population between the two sectors in order to promote a gradual expansion of industrial employment and output. Simultaneously, increases in agricultural productivity must be sufficient to permit a relatively smaller percentage of the total population to support the entire economy with food and raw materials.

THE DEVELOPED ECONOMIES

It is generally agreed that the economic development of what are now regarded as the developed economies originated some time during the eighteenth century. Much attention has been given to the role played in this developmental process by the so-called "Industrial Revolution", with its attendant inventions and the steady increases in productivity in the industrial sector.

The problem in the developed countries revolves around the question of whether the development process, to quote Demas (2, pp. 11–12), "ought to imply a fair degree of equality in per capita product and income between different *geographical regions* or between different *economic sectors* of the particular country". Both these aspects have been combined by Myrdal who asserts their necessity in order to attain "national economic integration" (32).

There was a high degree of complementarity between the agricultural and non-agricultural sectors during the developmental process in the developed economies. Initially, industrialization increased the demand for "wage-goods". In the early stages of development, food products were the most important goods in this category. This resulted in more favourable markets for agricultural products and stimulated crop and animal production on a cash basis.

However, improvements in agricultural productivity eventually have a heavy dependence on the availability (i.e. production by the non-agricultural sector) of sufficient fertilizers, tools, machines and other inputs required to take advantage of technological innovations. These inputs, in turn, further raise the productivity of the agricultural sector.

Industrialization also makes available to the population in the agricultural sector an increased volume and range of consumption goods. If the existence of these new goods raises the "wants" of the farm population in terms of consumption goods, then a further economic incentive is provided for greater productive effort in the agricultural sector.

The creation of more productive labour employment opportunities in the non-farm sector provides a means of diverting from agriculture labour which is underemployed because of the high productivity of the new forms of capital inputs being used in the agricultural sector. Such transfer, if labour resources are mobile, would benefit both those who leave the agricultural sector in those economies and those who remain in it, the latter by permitting the combination of greater quantities per capita of land and the newer capital inputs with the remaining members of the agricultural labour force.

Investment in education and research in many developed economies has led to the introduction of many new forms of reproducible capital inputs (e.g. fertilizers, pesticides, machinery, etc.) which can substitute for and increase the productivity of conventional agricultural resources. There have also been improvements in a number of conventional agricultural inputs which have increased their productivity also (e.g. improved seed varieties, breeds of animals, etc.). These new inputs and improved conventional inputs have had a high marginal product (high marginal rate of substitution) relative to other conventional inputs in the agricultural sector.

These new inputs have usually been produced by the non-agricultural sector and their supply has been highly elastic. Since the value of the marginal product of these inputs has been quite high relative to their price and since their supply elasticity to the agricultural sector has been quite high, these new inputs and improved conventional inputs have been readily introduced into the production process of the agricultural sector in most of the developed countries. Their introduction has also been facilitated by the fact that most of these new and improved inputs are highly divisible (e.g. fertilizers, spraying materials, better seed varieties, etc.). Furthermore, many such inputs require relatively little capital and so have been readily adopted. In addition, the supply of credit to agriculture has been relatively elastic in most developed countries, hence facilitating the adoption of some relatively more expensive new inputs.

The rapid adoption of these new and improved inputs by the agricultural sector has led to a substantial shift to the right of the supply function for farm products (as usually defined). This need not necessarily result in an over-supply of farm products or a depressed income in the agricultural sector (because of the demand for farm products being of less than unitary elasticity). The increased food production following the introduction of the new and improved inputs and the resultant fall in food prices would, through the market mechanism, bring about a readjustment of the quantities of other inputs in the agricultural sector, if there were free mobility of resources, until all inputs in the agricultural sector would obtain marginal returns comparable to those obtained by comparable inputs in the non-agricultural sector.

However, some conventional agricultural inputs have a very low short-run supply elasticity. Labour has a low supply elasticity to agriculture, due to such influences as values, training, lack of knowledge about alternative employment, etc. Much agricultural machinery is highly specialized to agricultural production and also depreciates slowly. These items have a high supply elasticity *into* agriculture. However, the short-run supply functions for these items are not reversible once these inputs have been added to the agricultural sector. In other words, many of these inputs also have an extremely low supply elasticity *out* of agriculture. Once these resources are committed to agriculture, they tend to remain and accept low-imputed returns.

Consequently, technological innovation resulting in the development of highly profitable new inputs and improved conventional inputs for use in the agricultural sector of most developed countries has led to rapid increases in farm output in the short run, with consequent reduction in the price of farm products since demand for farm products has not expanded to the same extent. Given that the price elasticity of demand for farm products is less than unitary, this has resulted in a decline in aggregate farm income in these countries. Thus the marginal value productivity and the imputed returns to the resources of low elasticity have declined. Much of the foregoing conceptualization draws heavily on research conducted by Heady and Tweeten (10).

This, then, is the problem of commercial agriculture in many of the developed countries. It has arisen because of the low supply-elasticity of certain resources in the farm sector. Its seriousness has been a matter of national concern in such countries because one of the resources with low supply elasticity in the agricultural sector is farm labour. Thus, agricultural incomes per capita tend to lie below the incomes of members of the non-farm labour force. Bellerby (1) has demonstrated the existence of large differences between relative incomes obtained by labour in agricultural and non-agricultural occupations in practically all countries. Even allowing for probable divergences of measured incomes from real incomes, Bellerby's data indicate that there is a difference in labour incomes in the two sectors.

Arising from this commercial farm problem there has been large-scale movement of labour out of agriculture. This movement of labour from agriculture has tended to be higher in certain areas than in others, depending partly on the extent to which the forces generating disequilibrium in agriculture acted on different areas and also on the extent to which the agricultural sectors of those areas experiencing the relatively greater disequilibria were enabled to adapt to the changing circumstances through resource adjustments.

In many cases, the movement of labour from agriculture has involved migration to local urban centres, to other urban centres within the same country or to emigration from the country involved, the latter phenomenon being of a relatively higher frequency in many European countries and in the less developed economies of the world.

As pointed out by Olson (34), other secularly declining industries from the employment point of view have existed in the advanced countries since World War II. The more notable in the United States have been the coal mining industry and the cotton textiles industry. Similarly in Great Britain and other European countries the coal mining industry has been exhibiting a secular decline in employment.

However, employment has also fallen substantially in the United States in such industries as the manufacture of earthenware food utensils. "Yet", as Olson reminds us, "the decline of these industries has not created nearly the rates of unemployment, or the extent of under-employment, or the social dislocations, or the political pressures that have characterized the declines of agriculture, coal mining and cotton textiles" (34, p. 985).

It appears obvious, therefore, that the industries which have, as they declined, left serious economic or social problems in their wake have been those which have dominated the communities in which they have been located. Coal mining had been a dominant industry in the Appalachian region of the United States and in certain regions of Europe now regarded as economically distressed areas. Textile manufacturing had been a major industry of many New England communities in the United States. Workers in these areas frequently lacked local alternative employment opportunities when these industries declined.

Similarly, in the case of agriculture, there has been a role of dominance in the economic affairs of many communities. "In the rural areas and in small country towns there are normally no enterprises apart from farms, and those businesses that sell capital inputs or consumption goods to farmers, or that market farm products. Thus when there is a secular decline in agriculture, there is normally also a secular decline in whatever other businesses exist in the farming area" (34, p. 986).

It is clear that as farm employment has declined, with the attendant decline in farm population and as transportation systems have improved, many small rural towns have lost a considerable degree of their *raison d'être*, hence contributing to the economically distressed area problem. The decline of Charlestown, one such town in the area covered by the present study, has been graphically portrayed by Healy (11).

Smith (37) has recently compared the problems and characteristics of many such areas with the characteristics of many of the underdeveloped economies of the world which are also in quest of industrialization. He has concluded that most of the problems involved in both types of area imply cost disadvantages of varying durations and magnitude to those who venture their capital in such areas.

In referring to the problems of industrial development in the less developed economies, he noted:

The list of problems has a monotonously familiar ring to those who have concerned themselves with the Appalachian area— lack of strategic categories of skilled labour, an inadequate supply of entrepreneurial and managerial skills, the sometimes irresponsible, unstable or incompetent local governments, poorly developed or non-existent industrial sites, poor transportation facilities and other items of social overhead capital, problems of market organization or market penetration in the domain of established brand names, developed technologies not suited to local resource configurations, etc. (37, p. 1228).

Considerable interest has been generated in the possibility of developing new industries in such predominantly rural areas to provide non-farm job opportunities for those people who would otherwise migrate to other areas for employment. It is claimed that this could enhance the development prospects of both agricultural and non-agricultural sectors in such areas.

The development of agriculture depends to a large extent on (a) investment which improves the level of farm technology and the quality of human and reproducible physical resources used in farming and (b) the efficient allocation and use of existing resources in agricultural communities. The development of local industrial activity can provide alternative employment opportunities for under-employed farm labour, both in the less developed economies and in those areas within the developed economies where such a problem exists.

By providing such alternative employment opportunities, a new source of income for farm investment and perhaps a new spirit of progress, local industrialization may set in motion a set of forces inducing higher levels of agricultural resource productivity, increased farm production, higher levels of farm family income and may also lead to a reduction in spatial and personal income inequality, thus contributing to Myrdal's "national economic integration".

3

Regional Industrial Development Policy in Ireland

Specific financial and other assistance designed to induce the establishment of industrial plants in Western Ireland was offered by the Irish Government following the passage of the Undeveloped Areas Act of 1952 (22). Section 3 of the Act delineates its area of application as (a) the congested districts (i.e. the area referred to in the last section) and (b) any other area to which, by order of the Minister for Industry and Commerce, the act is for the time being declared to apply. Any area to which the act applied was referred to as "an undeveloped area".

A board (An Foras Tionscal) was established and given wide powers to acquire land, way-leave or other land or water right (if necessary, by compulsory means), to construct, adapt and maintain buildings, to provide services in connection with land, to make grants to individuals to (a) acquire land, (b) construct, adapt and maintain buildings and other works, (c) acquire machinery and equipment for an industrial undertaking, (d) provide training (either in Ireland or abroad) of workers, to make grants where necessary for the provision of infra-structural elements, specifically the construction and repair of roads, bridges, harbour works and railway lines and facilities together with the provision of houses, canteens and other places of refreshment or recreation for persons employed in any such undertaking.

The goals and criteria of the new policy were set out in section 5 of the act, which states (22, p. 7):

For the purpose of providing and facilitating the provision of sites and premises for the establishment, development or maintenance in an underdeveloped area of an industrial undertaking in respect of which the Board are satisfied that—

(a) it would be likely to provide or maintain employment in such area, and

(b) financial assistance is necessary to ensure its establishment, maintenance or development, and

(c) it is of a reasonably permanent nature and will be carried on efficiently,

the Board may, on such terms as they think proper, ...

Some minor legislative amendments were contained in the Undeveloped Areas (Amendment) Act of 1957 (23), but this act dealt mainly with continuation of the legal powers of the board established under the 1952 act. Most of this act was subsequently repealed in 1963 by the Undeveloped Areas (Amendment) Act of 1963 (24). Separate grants for buildings and equipment were abolished and replaced by a single over-all grant. The maximum grant payable in the undeveloped areas set at two-thirds of the total estimated cost of a project where the total grant would not exceed £250,000. For projects in respect of which grants in excess of £250,000 were to be paid, the maximum was set at 50 per cent of estimated total cost or £1,000 per additional job expected by the board to be created as a result of the industrial project.

Excluding projects for which grants were approved but which did not proceed, a grant total of £10.472 million was approved for 165 projects in the undeveloped areas during the period from January 1952 to 31 March 1966 (20). The estimated employment expected to be directly generated by the projects for which grants were approved was 15,130. This represents a grant approval of £692 per estimated additional industrial worker. However, of the amount approved, slightly over £6.5 million had been paid out by 31 March 1966. Fennell (6) has estimated that the establishments to which £1.723 million was paid in grants up to March

1960 actually had an employment of 2,632 workers, representing a grant expenditure of nearly £650 per job.

Schemes to foster industrial development in Western Ireland are regarded by the Irish Government as a part of an over-all strategy to increase incomes in these areas. Referring to Western Ireland in the 1967 Budget Statement, the Irish Minister for Finance stated (21, p. 19):

Although every effort is being made to intensify agricultural development, the expansion of incomes of the rural community can be achieved only by a comprehensive development programme aimed at increasing employment and income derived from industry, tourism, angling, forestry and fishing as well as agriculture.

4

The Study Location

In an endeavour to select suitable sites for conducting the present study, Irish industrial and agricultural statistics pertaining to the West of Ireland were examined in detail. Certain criteria were established to aid in the area selection process. First of all, it was desired to study plants which had been located in predominantly rural labour market areas, in order to elicit information regarding industrialization effects on agriculture. Secondly, in order to enhance measurability of industrialization effects, preference was given to areas containing plants which had a reasonably large size of operation, in terms of labour force employed, relative to other non-farm employment on those areas.

It was also felt that plants which had exhibited a reasonably substantial rate of growth in employment during the previous five or six years would be most suited to the study. Furthermore, plants having a large proportion of males employed were sought, since the economic impact of such plants, especially on the farming sector, was expected to be greater than that of plants having a mainly female labour force.

Consideration was also given to the presence of natural geographic features which might facilitate the delineation around the plants to be studied of areas in which the bulk of the effects of the new plants might be expected to be felt. Ideally, it was desired to identify plants of reasonable size, located with the assistance of An Foras Tionscal, in places where formerly there was no other manufacturing activity and around which well-defined areas would be delineated such that confounding of effects would be minimized and measurement of effects facilitated.

On these bases, two areas were selected. One was around Tubbercurry, Co. Sligo, about 120 miles northwest of Dublin. The other area was around Scarriff, Co. Clare, which is about 120 miles west by southwest of Dublin.

These two areas are shaded in figure 1. Section A of this chapter contains a description of these two areas, while the new

Figure 1.   The study areas

industrial plants which were established in these areas are discussed in section B.

A.   THE TWO AREAS

1. The Tubbercurry area

The town of Tubbercurry is situated in the southwestern part of Co. Sligo. In 1956, Tubbercurry had a population of 933 persons.

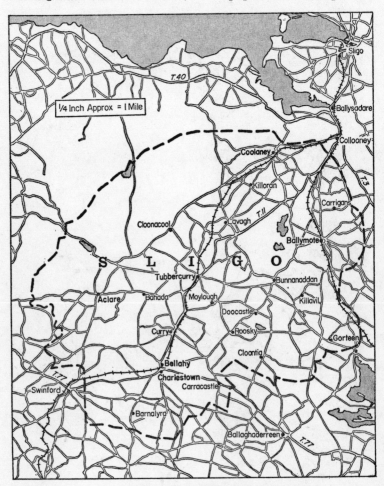

Figure 2. The Tubbercurry area

(Based on the Ordnance Survey by permission of the Government of the Republic of Ireland—Permit No. 997)

Population had declined to 878 by 1961, but by 1966 the population had risen to 937 persons.

Most of the land near Tubbercurry is between 200 and 400 feet above sea level. There are few level tracts of land in this lowland which is mainly composed of drumlin-drift terrain. Reference to figure 2 shows that to the west of Tubbercurry lie the Ox Mountains, a Caledonian ridge, varying in height from 600 to 1,800 feet above sea level and extending in a northeast–southwest direction. As stated by Freeman (7, p. 449),

. . . they form a clear population divide between the closely settled lowland on either side : the only important break is the Collooney gap, which carries the road and railway to Sligo. The mountains are a desolate expanse of spongy bog, which has a depth of 2 feet on the numerous massive erratics that occur on the high ground.

On the basis of preliminary information, an area was defined around Tubbercurry, such that it was expected to contain the residences of practically all of the plant employees. This area comprised the Rural District of Tubbercurry together with some additional adjoining district electoral divisions, a list of which is contained in Appendix A. For Irish census purposes, a "census town" is defined as a cluster of twenty or more occupied houses. The delineated area contained seven such towns of which the largest was Tubbercurry in 1966. These towns together had a 1966 population of 3,130 persons, a decline of 83 from the 1961 level. The total 1966 population of the area was 16,793 persons. Hence, the vast majority of the area's residents were farm and rural non-farm people.

Farms in the area are relatively small and are largely pastoral, cattle production being the predominant enterprise. In 1960, less than 3 per cent of the land in the Tubbercurry Rural District was under grain, root and green crops. Hay occupied about 9 per cent, while 46 per cent was under pasture. The other 42 per cent was classed as "other land", including woods, mountains, bogs, marshes, rivers, roads, etc. Total grain crops occupied 1.73 per cent of the land. Oats comprised 93 per cent of this acreage. Total root and green crops occupied 1.15 per cent of the land, about 94 per cent of the root and green crop acreage being devoted to potatoes.

The Rural District contained about 30,000 cattle, of which 25 per cent were milch cows. In addition there were about 3,000 pigs, 30,000 sheep and 1,000 horses.

Immediately prior to the establishment of the manufacturing plants on which the present study is based, there was no manufacturing activity in the Tubbercurry area. However, it was not always so. The celebrated chronicler of yesteryear, Arthur Young, visited the area in 1776 and reported that Lord Shelburne came to the area some 20 years previously, the area then being ". . . a wild uncultivated region, without industry or civility; and the people all roman catholicks, without an atom of manufactur, not even spinning" (40, p. 188).

Lord Shelburne then attempted to establish a weaving enterprise in Ballymote, but the project met with little success, as Lord Shelburne died shortly after its inception. In 1774, a Mr Fitzmaurice erected a bleachmill in Ballymote and installed looms, of which there were 90, when Young visited the area in 1776. Young observed that the 80 looms which were in operation in 1775

> . . . besides the 80 weavers, employed 80 persons more, which are usually women, quilling warping and winding; the quilling by children and half as many children for quilling; in all, 80 men, 80 women and 40 children (40, p. 190).

Subsequently, the plant expanded somewhat, but during the following century declined and, eventually, ceased operations.

2. The Scarriff area

The second location chosen was in the eastern part of County Clare. The town of Scarriff had a population of 698 persons in 1956, 600 in 1961 and 673 in 1966. As may be observed in figure 3, Scarriff is situated on the western edge of Lough Derg, one of the lakes on the River Shannon. Thus, this lake forms

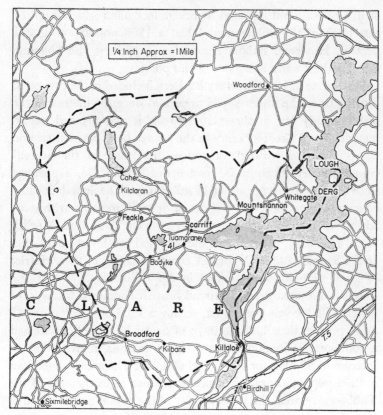

Figure 3.   The Scarriff area

(Based on the Ordnance Survey by permission of the Government of the Republic of Ireland—Permit No. 997)

quite an effective boundary on the eastern side of the area being delineated around Scarriff, since the first bridge across the Shannon to the south of Scarriff is at Killaloe, about 10 miles distant, while to the north of Scarriff, the lake extends to Portumna, Co. Galway, which is over 20 miles distant. On the northern side, the Slieve Aughty Mountains form an effective divide roughly coinciding with the Clare–Galway county boundary.

The town of Killaloe, situated on the west bank of the River Shannon, about 10 miles south of Scarriff, had a 1966 population of 816 persons and is joined by bridge to Ballina which is on the east bank of the Shannon and had a 1966 population of 271 persons. However, Ballina lies in Co. Tipperary, the Shannon forming the county boundary at this point.

Since none of Co. Tipperary has been included in the congested districts or in the undeveloped areas and since the interest of the present study lay in these latter areas, it was decided not to include any of Co. Tipperary in the area to be delineated around Scarriff. It was realized, of course, that some of the Scarriff employees were likely to be residents of Ballina, Co. Tipperary, since the two towns are about 11 miles apart. The area delineated contains the entire Rural District of Scarriff, together with some additional district electoral divisions (from Tulla and Meelick Rural Districts), which adjoin the west and southwest boundaries of the Scarriff Rural District. A complete listing of these district electoral divisions is contained in Appendix A.

In all, the area defined around Scarriff contained 6 towns, of which Killaloe was the largest, having a 1966 population of 143 more persons than had the town of Scarriff. These 6 towns had a combined 1966 population of 2,086 persons, representing an increase of 59 over the 1961 level of 2,027. The area defined had a 1966 population of 7,572 persons. Thus, as in the case of the Tubbercurry area, the vast majority of the population of the area were farm or rural non-farm residents.

The land utilization pattern of the Scarriff Rural District in 1960 showed some differences from that of the Tubbercurry Rural District. The land devoted to grain, root and green crops was slightly over 3 per cent of the total, slightly larger than the proportion in Tubbercurry. However, 1.21 per cent of the land was under grain crops, as opposed to 1.73 per cent in Tubbercurry, while 1.86 per cent consisted of root and green crops, compared with 1.15 per cent in Tubbercurry. Thus, root and green crops were relatively more prevalent than grain crops in Scarriff.

Further differences occur in the mix of grain crops and of root and green crops. Oats and potatoes were of relatively less importance in Scarriff, though still comprising the bulk of the grain, root and green crops. In Scarriff, oats constituted 70 per cent of the grain crop and potatoes accounted for 60 per cent of the root and green crop acreage, compared with the corresponding figures of 93 per cent and 94 per cent, respectively, which were noted earlier in the Tubbercurry Rural District.

Hay (13 per cent) occupies a greater proportion of the land than in Tubbercurry (9 per cent). The amount under pasture (47 per cent) is also slightly larger while the proportion of "other land" (37 per cent) is correspondingly less than in the Tubbercurry Rural District (47 per cent).

The Scarriff Rural District contained about 30,000 cattle, less than 2,000 pigs and less than 10,000 sheep in 1960. However, the number of horses was greater than in Tubbercurry. The uplands in the area have some sheep farming, but the raising of cattle is again of greater importance throughout the area.

Industrial activity (other than at the plant under study) is rather sparse in the area. In Scarriff itself, there is a creamery. Nearby, there are some sawmilling operations, while in Killaloe there is a weaving enterprise in which the employees are mainly females. Based mainly in Killaloe, a fairly important and expanding tourist industry has been developing recently in association with the development of Lough Derg as a resort area.

B.   THE NEW PLANTS

1. Tubbercurry

During the year ended 31 March 1956, Basta, Limited received approval for a grant of £20,000 from An Foras Tionscal to establish a plant in Tubbercurry for the manufacture of locks, etc. (13). The grant was paid during the same year and the plant commenced operations. As part of its requirements, this plant needed tooling services, so a small workshop was subsequently set up to provide the required tooling services.

As the latter operation continued to grow, it was decided to incorporate it as another company. Thus, The Tool and Gauge

Company of Ireland, Limited came into being, and during 1959–60 received approval for a grant of £58,600 from An Foras Tionscal (14). Grant payments to this company in 1959–60 amounted to £25,300 (14). During 1960–61, the company received £11,205 (15), while a further £3,000 was paid to them in 1961–62 (16). During 1963–64 the grant paid was £10,300 (18), another £2,400 being paid during 1964–65 (19). The balance of £6,395 of the original £58,600 which was approved during 1959–60 was paid to the company during 1965–66 (20).

The Tool and Gauge Company of Ireland, Limited provides all the tooling required by Basta, Limited. In addition, however, the company has developed a large volume of business with other firms requiring tooling and allied equipment. The company provides a large range of press tools, jigs, fixtures, gauges and moulds to a variety of industries and also to diesinkers and machine engravers.

As a result of the increased requirements both of Basta, Limited and of The Tool and Gauge Company of Ireland, Limited for metal castings, it was decided more recently to incorporate a third company, Irish Industrial Foundries Company, Limited. This third company received approval during 1965–66 for a £100,000 grant from An Foras Tionscal (20), £24,000 of which was paid to the company during 1965–66. The new company is to engage in the production of plumbers' brassware, castings, etc.

The plants operated by these three companies, which may be regarded as outgrowths of a single industrial development, are all located in close proximity to one another in the same part of Tubbercurry. Hence, in analysing the direct effects of these plants on the Tubbercurry area, they may be considered as one.

Apart from sales among themselves, practically all of the products manufactured by the plants located in Tubbercurry are exported from the area. Some sales are made to other Irish firms, but there is a growing volume of sales to places outside Ireland.

Hence, direct effects of these new plants on the Tubbercurry area might be expected to occur almost wholly through the purchase of inputs by the new firms from local suppliers. Inputs required by these plants include labour services, metal in various forms, plastic for moulds, certain lock components, etc. Practically all of these inputs, except labour services, are purchased from sources outside the area. Hence, the direct effects on the area would be almost exclusively generated by the hiring of labour services from within the area.

When the study was conducted in 1966, the plants had a combined employment of 183 persons up through the rank of working foreman, including office personnel but excluding management personnel. Total employment at the Tubbercurry plants had reached about 30 by 1958 and grew steadily until 1961 when the number of employees was over 200. Since then, employment at the plants has tended to fluctuate somewhat within the range of 180 to 210.

Using the size classification proposed by Staley and Morse (38, p. 14), in which industrial firms having less than 10 employees are classed as *very small*, those having 10 and less than 100 classed as *small* and those having 100 and less than 250 employees are classed as *medium*, it is to be noted that each of the three Tubbercurry plants is in the *small* category. Hence, in combination, they may be considered as three *small* plants. However, since the impact of all three is to be examined as if they were one establishment, the three plants together may be regarded as one *medium*-sized industrial undertaking.

2. Scarriff

A grant of £314,000 was approved by An Foras Tionscal during 1959–60 for the establishment of a plant in Scarriff by Chipboard, Limited (14). Of this amount, £191,000 was paid to the new firm during 1959–60, £19,000 during 1960–61 (15), £10,500 during 1961–62 (16), £3,500 during 1962–63 (17) and £45,000 during 1963–64 (18), while the balance of £45,000 from the original grant approved was paid to the firm during 1964–65 (19).

As its name implies, Chipboard, Limited is engaged in the

manufacture of chipboard, which is used extensively by the building trade. A large volume of production is exported from Ireland, mainly from a port on the east coast. As the product is quite heavy relative to value, the transportation costs involved are rather large. The company has acquired its own fleet of lorries which haul the chipboard over the 120 or so miles to the port.

Partly in response to this cost situation, Chipboard, Limited has recently commenced further processing of some of the chipboard into veneered and plastic-faced chipboard for use in higher quality kitchen units, etc. Towards this end, An Foras Tionscal during 1965–66 approved an "adaptation grant" of £43,500 to Chipboard, Limited (20). Most of this grant was paid to the company during 1965–66.

Scarcely any of the products manufactured by Chipboard, Limited are sold within the area. Hence, once again, the direct effects of the new plant would be expected to occur *via* factor demand. Inputs required by Chipboard, Limited include labour services, timber, glue, plastic, etc. Some, but not much, timber is acquired within the area; currently, the firm acquires timber from a wide geographical area. Practically all of the non-labour inputs are purchased from suppliers outside the area. Thus, the direct effects of Chipboard, Limited on the Scarriff area would occur almost entirely as a result of the hiring of labour services from within the area.

When this study was conducted in 1966, Chipboard, Limited had 194 employees up through the rank of working foreman, including office personnel. Management personnel were excluded from this count. Employment at the plant was initially about 80 during 1960. About 50 more employees were added in the following year and employment at the plant has since grown rather steadily to its current level. Hence, it is seen that this plant also falls, according to the Staley and Morse classification, into the *medium*-sized category.

5

The Plant Employees

This chapter contains a descriptive analysis of the labour force of the industrial plants in the two areas. Certain personal and household characteristics of the plant employees are discussed in sections A and B, while section C focuses on characteristics of the present employment of these employees. In view of the special interest of this study in the employment of farm people at the new plants, personal and farm business characteristics of farm operators who obtained plant employment are examined in section D.

A.   EMPLOYEE CHARACTERISTICS

In July 1966, the Tubbercurry factories had 183 employees up through the rank of working foreman, while the Scarriff factory had 194 such employees. In addition, each factory had a group of management personnel. Interviews were obtained with 157 employees in Tubbercurry and with 151 employees in Scarriff. Twenty-five of those not interviewed in Scarriff were either timber-workers or lorry drivers who were not available for interview. Various personal characteristics of the employees interviewed are described in this section.

1.   Sex

As lists of all plant employees were supplied by the factory management personnel, it was possible to determine the sex of all plant employees in each area. Hence, in table 1, which contains

the distribution of plant employees by sex, data are presented
regarding all the plant employees and in regard to those plant

TABLE 1. Distribution of plant employees by sex

	Tubbercurry		Scarriff	
	Number	Per cent	Number	Per cent
Total employees				
Male	138	75.4	184	94.8
Female	45	24.6	10	5.2
Total	183	100.0	194	100.0
Employees interviewed				
Male	116	73.9	142	94.0
Female	41	26.1	9	6.0
Total	157	100.0	151	100.0

TABLE 2. Distribution of plant employees by age

	Tubbercurry		Scarriff	
	Number	Per cent	Number	Per cent
Under 15	1	0.7	—	—
15 and under 20	48	30.5	14	9.3
20 and under 25	52	33.1	40	26.5
25 and under 30	17	10.8	20	13.3
30 and under 35	11	7.0	15	9.9
35 and under 40	8	5.1	18	11.9
40 and under 45	11	7.0	15	9.9
45 and under 50	3	1.9	10	6.6
50 and under 55	3	1.9	9	6.0
55 and under 60	1	0.7	6	4.0
60 and over	2	1.3	4	2.6
Total	157	100.0	151	100.0
Mean age	25.6		32.8	
Median age	21		30	
Modal age	19		20	

employees who were interviewed in connection with the present study. Forty-five of the Tubbercurry employees (about 25 per cent) were females, while there were 10 females (slightly over 5 per cent) employed at the Scarriff plant. 26 per cent of the employees interviewed in Tubbercurry were females, while 6 per cent of those interviewed at the Scarriff plant were females. Thus, the proportion of males and females in the sample of plant employees interviewed was about the same as that obtained among all plant employees.

2. Age

Plant employees are classified by age in table 2. In general, the Tubbercurry employees were younger than the Scarriff employees, the mean age of the former group being 25.6, while that of the latter group was 32.8 years. The median age of Tubbercurry employees was 21 years, 9 years lower than the median age of Scarriff employees. Similarly the modal age was also lower in Tubbercurry than in Scarriff. These data regarding age were obtained during the interviews with plant employees.

3. Marital status

Information obtained during the interviews regarding the marital status of the plant employees is contained in table 3. 37 per cent of the male employees aged 18 years and over in Tubbercurry were married, while 45 per cent of the male employees aged 18 years and over in Scarriff were married. All but one of the female employees in Tubbercurry were unmarried, while none of the female employees in Scarriff was married. As there was a much higher proportion of females employed in Tubbercurry than in Scarriff, it is seen that 38 or 28 per cent of the employees aged 18 years and over who were interviewed in Tubbercurry were married, while the corresponding number of married employees interviewed in Scarriff was 63 or 43 per cent. It is thus seen that the labour force of the new industrial plants in both areas consisted largely of unmarried people, with about 40 per

TABLE 3. Marital status of plant employees by sex

Marital Status	Tubercurry				Scarriff			
	Male		Female		Male		Female	
	Number	Per cent	Number	Per cent	Number	Per cent	Number	Per cent
Married	37	37.4	1	2.9	63	45.0	—	—
Single	61	61.6	34	97.1	77	55.0	8	100.0
Widowed	1	1.0	—	—	—	—	—	—
Subtotal	99	100.0	35	100.0	140	100.0	8	100.0
Employees under 18 years	17	—	6	—	2	—	1	—
Total	116	—	41	—	142	—	9	—

cent of the male employees being married and practically all of the female employees unmarried.

4. Educational attainment

The level of education attained by the plant employees who were interviewed was quite different in the two areas, as shown in table 4. Over 63 per cent of the Scarriff employees received no

TABLE 4. Educational attainment of plant employees

Level of Education	Tubbercurry		Scarriff	
	Number	Per cent	Number	Per cent
Primary only	55	35.0	96	63.5
Primary + secondary	23	14.6	11	7.3
Primary + vocational	66	42.2	35	23.2
Primary + secondary + vocational	12	7.6	6	4.0
Primary + secondary + university	—	—	2	1.3
Primary + secondary + other	1	0.6	—	—
Primary + vocational + other	—	—	1	0.7
Total	157	100.0	151	100.0

education beyond the primary level, as compared with 35 per cent in Tubbercurry. Of those receiving post-primary education, the vast majority had attended vocational schools. Some had attended secondary schools, while a few employees had attended vocational schools after one or more years of secondary school attendance. In all, about 50 per cent of the Tubbercurry employees had some vocational school education, while less than 30 per cent of the Scarriff employees had attended vocational schools. Differences in educational attainment by sex were slight. For example 51 per cent of the male employees in Tubbercurry had attended vocational school, while 46 per cent of the female employees had done so.

Examination of the number of years of post-primary education obtained by plant employees reveals that the most frequently occurring quantity of post-primary education among those obtaining such education was 3 years for the Tubbercurry employees and 2 years for the Scarriff employees. The basic course of study in the vocational schools was one of two years duration, at the end of which period of study a state examination for the Group Certificate was administered to pupils.[1] It was then possible for pupils who wished to study further for a trade to spend an additional year of study at a vocational school. This third year was largely a "practical year" and was frequently combined with an apprenticeship program for the trade in which the pupils were interested. It would appear, from the data contained in table 5, that most of the plant employees in the Scarriff area who had

TABLE 5. Distribution of plant employees by number of years post-primary education

Years Post Primary Education	Tubbercurry		Scarriff	
	Number	Per cent	Number	Per cent
0	55	35.0	96	63.5
1	13	8.3	6	4.0
2	20	12.7	18	11.9
3	34	21.7	16	10.6
4	16	10.2	3	2.0
5	13	8.3	7	4.6
6	2	1.3	1	0.7
7	2	1.3	3	2.0
8	1	0.6	1	0.7
9	1	0.6	—	—
Total	157	100.0	151	100.0
Mean number of years of post-primary education	2.08		1.14	

attended vocational school had done so for the basic two-year course. In the Tubbercurry area, on the other hand, the majority of those attending vocational school had done so for three years. This difference would be associated with higher levels of skill

[1] Since the present study was completed, the time-structure of vocational education has been changed somewhat.

requirement for certain positions in the Tubbercurry plants and with the apprenticeship program which was developed to satisfy partly these requirements, thus providing a greater opportunity to residents of the Tubbercurry area for the acquisition and subsequent use of such skills.

As shown in table 5, 44 per cent of the Tubbercurry employees received three or more years of post-primary education, while about 20 per cent of the Scarriff employees received this amount of education. The mean number of years of post-primary education received by plant employees was 2.08 in Tubbercurry and 1.14 in Scarriff. These educational differences are largely due to the hiring policies of the new firms, arising from the requirements of the particular jobs offered. In Tubbercurry, there was a greater demand for skilled employees, who would have higher levels of training. Similarly, a large number of apprentices was recruited. These also would have vocational school training.

5. Farm association: residence

Plant employees are classified in table 6 according to whether they resided in farm, non-farm rural or urban households. All

TABLE 6. Distribution of plant employees by type of residence

Type of Residence	Tubbercurry		Scarriff	
	Number	Per cent	Number	Per cent
Farm	94	59.9	60	39.8
Non-farm Rural	11	7.0	20	13.2
Urban	52	33.1	71	47.0
Total	157	100.0	151	100.0

employees residing in "census towns" (defined as clusters of 20 or more occupied houses) are classed as urban residents. The number of plant employees residing on farms was much larger in Tubbercurry, amounting to 60 per cent as opposed to 40 per cent in Scarriff. About one third of the Tubbercurry employees were urban residents, while nearly half of the Scarriff employees resided in towns. In both areas a small portion of plant employees were rural non-farm residents.

6. Farm association: work

All employees were classified by their farm work association. A farm operator was defined as a person who did some farm work (apart from maintenance) on fifty or more days during the preceding year, who was paid from farm profits (i.e. did not receive a fixed wage) and who made the management decisions regarding what crops were grown and what livestock were kept on that farm. All other farm workers were classed as non-operator farm workers. These latter failed to meet one or more of the above criteria, but worked on a farm. In classifying people as non-operator farm workers a lower limit of twenty days on which some farm work was done was applied. This procedure was followed in order to exclude from the non-operator farm worker category those people who might help at farm work during periods of peak labour demands and those who might just do some farm work during vacations from other employment.

The distribution of plant employees by farm work association is shown in table 7, which contains data regarding the farm work association of plant employees both immediately prior to their obtaining employment at the new industrial plants and when interviewed in connection with the present study. Because of the criteria used, it transpired that the number of farm operators actually employed at both plants was lower than expected on the basis of preliminary enquiries. Many of those originally thought to be farm operators were, in fact, non-operator farm workers. Failure to satisfy the third criterion, that of responsibility for management decisions on the farm, was the most frequent cause for reclassification of those who had been felt to be farm operators on the basis of preliminary information.

In Tubbercurry, 15 plant employees were farm operators at the time of obtaining industrial employment and were still farm operators when the present study was conducted, as compared

TABLE 7. Distribution of plant employees by farm work association

Farm work association	Tubbercurry		Scarriff	
	Number	Per cent (n = 157)	Number	Per cent (n = 151)
Farm operator at time of taking plant employment and is farm operator now	15	9.6	17	11.3
Farm operator at time of taking plant employment and is non-operator farm worker now	—	—	1	0.7
Non-operator farm worker at time of taking plant employment and is farm operator now	1	0.6	1	0.7
Non-operator farm worker at time of taking plant employment and is non-operator farm worker now	46	29.3	31	20.5
Non-operator farm worker at time of taking plant employment and has no farm work association now	18	11.5	12	7.9
No farm work association on taking plant employment and is farm operator now	—	—	1	0.7
No farm work association on taking plant employment and is non-operator farm worker now	4	2.5	1	0.7
No farm work association on taking plant employment and has no farm work association now	73	46.5	87	57.6

with 17 such farm operators in Scarriff. One farm operator in Scarriff had ceased to be a farm operator at some stage subsequent to employment at the new plant and was a non-operator farm worker at the time of interview. In Scarriff, also, one person, who at the time of employment had no farm work association, subsequently became a farm operator, while, in both areas, one person who was originally a non-operator farm worker became a farm operator subsequent to obtaining employment at the new plant.

65 of the Tubbercurry employees (41.4 per cent) were non-operator farm workers when hired at the new plant. 18 of these (28 per cent) subsequently ceased to have any farm work association. In Scarriff, 44 plant employees (29.1 per cent) were originally non-operator farm workers, 12 of whom (27 per cent) later ceased to have any farm work association. This was the most frequently occurring movement among types of farm work association following employment at the new industrial plants. A few people who had no farm work association when hired at the new plants subsequently became non-operator farm workers.

In all, when the present study was conducted, 16 employees (10.2 per cent) in Tubbercurry and 19 employees (12.6 per cent) in Scarriff were farm operators. Fifty employees (31.8 per cent) in Tubbercurry and 33 employees (21.8 per cent) in Scarriff were non-operator farm workers, while, in both areas, the majority of plant employees, 91 or 58.0 per cent in Tubbercurry and 99 or 65.6 per cent in Scarriff had no farm work association when this study was conducted.

B. HOUSEHOLD CHARACTERISTICS

In the present section, certain attributes of the households of plant employees are described, along with the plant employees' status within their households.

1. Status within household

As seen from table 8, slightly over half of the Scarriff employees were heads of households, while in Tubbercurry about 30 per cent of the plant employees were heads of households. This difference is largely due to the fact that, as noted earlier, married males

TABLE 8. Status of plant employees within their households

Household status	Tubbercurry		Scarriff	
	Number	Per cent	Number	Per cent
Head of household	47	29.9	77	51.0
Other household member	110	70.1	74	49.0
Total	157	100.0	151	100.0

formed a much larger proportion of the plant employees in Scarriff than in Tubbercurry.

The relationship of the other plant employees to the heads of the households wherein they resided is shown in table 9. The most

TABLE 9. Relationships of plant employees to heads of households in which they resided

Relationship to head	Tubbercurry		Scarriff	
	Number	Per cent	Number	Per cent
Wife	1	0.9	—	—
Son, son-in-law, stepson	67	61.0	61	82.4
Daughter, daughter-in-law, step-daughter	38	34.5	6	8.1
Brother, brother-in-law, stepbrother	1	0.9	3	4.1
Other relation	3	2.7	4	5.4
Subtotal	110	100.0	74	100.0
Heads of households	47	—	77	—
Total	157	—	151	—

frequently occurring relationship to the head of the household was that of son, son-in-law or stepson, accounting for over 60 per cent of the other household members employed in Tubbercurry and for over 80 per cent of those in Scarriff. In all, the two relationship groups, son, son-in-law or stepson and daughter, daughter-in-law or stepdaughter, accounted for nearly 95 per cent of the other household members employed in Tubbercurry and for over 90 per cent of those in Scarriff.

TABLE 10. Distribution of all plant employees and of households containing these employees by number of employees per household

Employees per household	Tubbercurry				Scarriff			
	Employees		Households		Employees		Households	
	Number	Per cent	Number	Per cent	Number	Per cent	Number	Per cent
One	143	78.1	143	87.7	161	83.0	161	91.4
Two	40	21.9	20	12.3	26	13.4	13	7.4
Three	—	—	—	—	3	1.5	1	0.6
Four	—	—	—	—	4	2.1	1	0.6
Total	183	100.0	163	100.0	194	100.0	176	100.0

Thus, in Tubbercurry, about 30 per cent of plant employees were heads of households, the remainder being nearly all sons or daughters of heads of households, while in Scarriff about half of the plant employees were heads of households, most of the other half also being sons or daughters.

2. Multi-employee households

Some households in both areas contained more than one plant employee. The term multi-employee household is used to refer to such households. In some of these households, the head was employed at the plant along with one or more other members, while in other cases the head was not employed at the plant but two or more other members were. It was possible from the lists of employees to ascertain in respect of all employees whether or not they belonged to multi-employee households.

In Tubbercurry, as shown in table 10, 40 employees or 22 per cent came from households with two members employed at the plant. Hence, the total number of households containing plant employees was 163. In Scarriff, 26 employees came from two-employee households. There was also one three-employee household and one four-employee household. Hence, the number of households containing Scarriff plant employees was 176.

Similar information is presented in table 11 regarding the employees who were interviewed in both areas. 36 or 23 per cent of the 157 employees interviewed in Tubbercurry were members of multi-employee households, while in Scarriff 25 employees or 16.5 per cent of those interviewed were members of multi-employee households.

3. Number of people in household

Table 12 shows the distribution by household size of the plant employees who were interviewed. There is hardly any difference between the two groups of employees in this respect. For example, 36 per cent of the Tubbercurry employees and 35 per cent of the Scarriff employees were members of households containing 3 or

TABLE 11. Distribution of plant employees interviewed and their households by number of employees per household

| Employees per household | Tubbercurry | | | | Scarriff | | | |
| | Employees | | Households | | Employees | | Households | |
	Number	Per cent	Number	Per cent	Number	Per cent	Number	Per cent
One	121	77.1	121	85.8	126	83.5	126	89.4
Two	36	22.9	20	14.2	19	12.6	13	9.2
Three	—	—	—	—	2	1.3	1	0.7
Four	—	—	—	—	4	2.6	1	0.7
Total	157	100.0	141	100.0	151	100.0	141	100.0

TABLE 12. Distribution of plant employees by number of people in the households of which they were members

Size of household (people)	Tubbercurry		Scarriff	
	Number	Per cent	Number	Per cent
1	9	5.7	11	7.3
2	18	11.5	16	10.6
3	30	19.1	26	17.2
4	33	21.0	26	17.2
5	25	15.9	26	17.2
6	11	7.0	24	15.9
7	14	8.9	11	7.3
8	5	3.2	1	0.7
9	8	5.1	7	4.6
10	2	1.3	2	1.3
11	2	1.3	1	0.7
Total	157	100.0	151	100.0

fewer members. The proportion of plant employees residing in households containing 4, 5 or 6 members was somewhat higher in Scarriff, while the proportion of employees who were members of households containing 7 or more members was slightly higher in Tubbercurry than in Scarriff. The distribution by household size

TABLE 13. Distribution of households containing one or more plant employees by size of household

Size of household (people)	Tubbercurry		Scarriff	
	Number	Per cent	Number	Per cent
1	9	6.4	11	7.8
2	17	12.1	16	11.4
3	27	19.2	25	17.7
4	31	22.0	26	18.4
5	21	14.9	23	16.3
6	11	7.8	20	14.2
7	13	9.2	10	7.1
8	4	2.8	1	0.7
9	5	3.5	6	4.3
10	2	1.4	2	1.4
11	1	0.7	1	9.7
Total	141	100.0	141	100.0

of the households which contain one or more plant employees is shown in table 13. In both areas the median size of households which contained plant employees was 4 persons. In Tubbercurry, 38 per cent of the households containing plant employees had three or fewer members, the corresponding fraction for Scarriff being 36 per cent. About 45 per cent of the Tubbercurry households had 4, 5 or 6 members while 49 per cent of the Scarriff households fell in this size-range. Households containing 7 or more members amounted to slightly more than 17 per cent of the Tubbercurry group and about 14 per cent of the Scarriff group of households which contained plant members.

4. Family-classification of households

Plant employees were grouped according to the family classification of their households. This grouping is shown in table 14. In Tubbercurry, 113 employees or 72 per cent of the total interviewed were members of husband-wife family households where both spouses were present. A further 18.5 per cent were members

TABLE 14. Distribution of plant employees by family-classification of their households

Family Classification	Tubbercurry		Scarriff	
	Number	Per cent	Number	Per cent
Husband-wife family household: both spouses present	113	71.9	112	74.2
Broken-family household: one spouse present, mother and child(ren), or father and child(ren)	29	18.5	16	10.6
Non-conjugal family household: brothers, brothers and sisters, etc.	5	3.2	9	5.9
Single person household	10	6.4	14	9.3
Total	157	100.0	151	100.0

of broken-family households, where the head of the household was either widowed or separated (legally or informally) from his/her spouse. Five plant employees were members of non-conjugal family households, for example, brothers and sisters or aunts, uncles, nephews and nieces living in one household. A further 10 people were members of single-person households.

In Scarriff, a somewhat higher proportion of employees belonged to husband-wife family households. Considerably less Scarriff employees were members of broken-family households. The number of employees who resided in non-conjugal family households and in single person households was, however, larger in Scarriff than in Tubbercurry.

To facilitate comparisons on a household basis, table 15 shows the distribution by family classification of households in both

TABLE 15. Distribution by family-classification of households containing one or more plant employees

Family Classification	Tubbercurry		Scarriff	
	Number	Per cent	Number	Per cent
Husband-wife family household: both spouses present	102	72.4	102	72.4
Broken-family household: one spouse present, mother and child(ren), or father and child(ren)	24	17.0	16	11.3
Non-conjugal family household: brothers, brothers and sisters, etc.	5	3.5	9	6.4
Single person household	10	7.1	14	9.9
Total	141	100.0	151	100.0

areas which contain one or more plant employees. Exactly the same proportion of households containing plant employees (72.4 per cent) were husband-wife family households in each area. On a household basis, single-person households as a proportion of households containing plant employees numbered 7.1 per cent in Tubbercurry and 9.9 per cent in Scarriff.

Thus, about three quarters of the households containing plant employees in both areas were husband-wife family households, the remaining households having other family combinations or else being single person households.

C.   EMPLOYMENT CHARACTERISTICS

This section contains a description of the plant employees' jobs, how these jobs were obtained and the length of time plant employees held their present jobs prior to the study being conducted.

1. Present occupation

The plant employees who were interviewed are classified by present occupation in table 16. Some occupations are exclusive to each plant. However, there is a certain overlap in the occupational breakdown of plant employees in both areas, particularly since a relatively large proportion of the plant employees fell in the unskilled labour category. Over 34 per cent of the employees interviewed in Tubbercurry were classed as general labourer or other unskilled worker, while 68 or 45 per cent of those interviewed in Scarriff were so classed.

22 or 14 per cent of those interviewed in Tubbercurry were apprentices, as compared with 3 employees or 2 per cent in Scarriff. As can be inferred from this, a rather large apprenticeship program has been introduced in Tubbercurry in an effort to increase the supply of skilled labour to the plant. Clerical personnel amounted to about 10 per cent of those interviewed in Tubbercurry and about 8 per cent in Scarriff.

2. Manner of recruitment

The manner in which plant employees obtained their present employment is shown in table 17. By far the majority of plant employees in both areas obtained their employment by just applying at the plant office. Nearly 70 per cent of the Tubber-

TABLE 16. Distribution of plant employees by present occupation

Present occupation	Tubbercurry		Scarriff	
	Number	Per cent	Number	Per cent
Fitter, assembler or mechanic	3	1.9	5	3.3
Diecaster	5	3.2	—	—
Other skilled metal worker	7	4.5	2	1.3
Metal working machinist	3	1.9	—	—
Apprentice	22	14.0	3	2.0
Warehouser or packer	10	6.4	5	3.3
Other commercial worker	1	0.6	1	0.7
Other service worker	1	0.6	3	2.0
Other professional or technical worker	4	2.6	2	1.3
Foreman or supervisor	9	5.7	8	5.3
Clerk or typist	16	10.2	12	7.8
General labourer or other unskilled worker	54	34.4	68	45.1
Carpenter or joiner	—	—	3	2.0
Sawyer or other woodworking machinist	—	—	13	8.6
Building tradesman	—	—	4	2.6
Veneerer or finisher	—	—	6	4.0
Saw doctor	—	—	1	0.7
Skilled electrical worker	—	—	3	2.0
Operator of moving machinery	—	—	4	2.6
Operator of crane, stationary engine, etc.	—	—	3	2.0
Truck driver	—	—	4	2.6
Other transport and communications worker	—	—	1	0.7
Total	157	100.0	151	100.0

curry employees and over 65 per cent of the Scarriff employees obtained their present positions in this manner. The next most frequent response in both areas was that the employee heard of the availability of this job from a friend or relative. In many of these cases, a relative of the present employee had been working at the plant and had obtained employment for other members of his household or other relatives. Occasionally, when one employee left the plant's employ, a close relative of his might come to work at the plant to "replace him".

The third most frequent manner of recruitment in both areas

TABLE 17. Distribution of plant employees by manner of recruitment to present employment

Manner of recruitment	Tubbercurry		Scarriff	
	Number	Per cent	Number	Per cent
Newspaper advertisement	11	7.0	9	6.9
Just applied at the plant office	108	68.8	99	65.5
Heard of job from friend or relative	20	12.7	25	16.6
Through private employment agency	3	1.9	1	0.7
Contacted by employer	15	9.6	17	11.2
Total	157	100.0	151	100.0

involved the employer seeking out and contacting the potential employee. In Tubbercurry, 15 or nearly 10 per cent of the plant employees were recruited in this manner, while, in Scarriff, 17 or 11 per cent of the employees were so recruited. 7 per cent of the Tubbercurry employees and 6 per cent of the Scarriff employees were recruited by newspaper advertisement, while, in both areas, recruitment through an employment agency or placing service was negligible.

3. Length of time in present position

Plant employees were classified according to the length of time during which they had worked at the new plants. This classification is shown in table 18. Because of its longer period of operation, the Tubbercurry plant had some employees who had worked there for over 8 years. Both plants had a fairly similar distribution of employees among the other categories of length of employee service. In Scarriff, 28 employees had worked at the plant for less than one year prior to the survey, the same number as in Tubbercurry. In Tubbercurry, 85 employees or 54.2 per cent had been employed for less than 3 years, as compared with 82 or 54.3 per cent in Scarriff. Largely because of increased length of plant operation in Tubbercurry, the mean number of months of employment was 45.9 in Tubbercurry and 41.0 in Scarriff.

TABLE 18. Distribution of plant employees by length of time in present position

Number of Months	Tubbercurry		Scarriff	
	Number	Per cent	Number	Per cent
Under 3	3	1.9	7	4.6
3 and under 6	4	2.5	15	9.9
6 and under 9	7	4.5	2	1.3
9 and under 12	14	8.9	4	2.6
12 and under 18	8	5.1	4	2.6
18 and under 24	11	7.0	11	7.3
24 and under 30	16	10.2	12	7.9
30 and under 36	9	5.7	14	9.3
36 and under 48	16	10.2	21	14.0
48 and under 60	20	12.7	17	11.3
60 and under 72	19	12.1	19	12.6
72 and under 84	7	4.5	11	7.3
84 and under 96	5	3.2	13	8.6
96 and over	18	11.5	1	0.7
Total	157	100.0	151	100.0
Mean number of months	45.9		41.0	

The major contrast between the two areas arose when the duration of employment was classified by farm work association. Plant employees who were farm operators before accepting employment at the new plant and who remained farm operators following such employment had a mean duration of employment of 80.5 months in Tubbercurry and 36.6 months in Scarriff. This indicates that the farm operators were nearly all hired in the early stages of plant operation in Tubbercurry but that in Scarriff their hiring was more scattered throughout the period of operation of the plant.

D. FARM OPERATOR PLANT EMPLOYEES

In this section, certain personal and farm business characteristics of those farm operators who obtained employment at the new plants and who did not subsequently change their farm work association are examined.

1. Personal characteristics

In both areas all of the farm operators who were employed at the new plants were males. 14 of the 15 farm operators employed in Tubbercurry were heads of households. The other farm operator was the son of the head of the household in which he resided. 14 of the 17 farm operators employed at the Scarriff plant were heads of households. 2 of the remaining 3 were sons of the heads of the households in which they resided, while the third was a nephew of the head of his household.

All but one of the 15 farm operators employed in Tubbercurry were members of one-employee households. Similarly, all but one of the 17 farm operators employed at the Scarriff plant were members of one-employee households.

11 of the 15 farm operators employed in Tubbercurry were married, while 11 of the 17 farm operators employed at the Scarriff plant were married.

The mean age of the farm operators employed in Tubbercurry was 41 years. The mean age of farm operators employed at the Scarriff plant was 36.9 years.

7 of the 15 farm operators employed in Tubbercurry had received some education beyond the primary school level. Most of these people had attended vocational school. The mean number of years of post-primary education obtained by the farm operator plant employees in Tubbercurry was 1.47 years.

In contrast, only 3 of the 17 farm operators employed at the Scarriff plant had received any post-primary education. The mean number of years of post-primary education received by the Scarriff farm operator plant employees was 0.3 years.

2. Farm business characteristics

Farm business characteristics of those farm operators who accepted plant employment and who did not subsequently change their farm work association are described hereunder. This description focuses on land utilization, livestock enterprises, labour use, machinery use and farm income.

a. Land utilization

Land utilization of farm operator plant employees in both areas is shown in table 19. Those farm operators employed in Tubbercurry operated a mean acreage of 30.067, while their Scarriff

TABLE 19. 1966 land utilization pattern of farm operator plant employees

Characteristic (mean)	Tubbercurry (n = 15)	Scarriff (n = 17)
Total acres operated	30.067	34.117
Wheat	.059	—
Oats	.741	.573
Barley	.029	.053
Total grain crops	.829	.627
Potatoes	.433	.924
Other root and green crops	.187	.511
Total root and green crops	.620	1.435
Hay	6.140	9.059
Pasture	21.767	20.524
Woods and plantations	.013	.029
Other land	.900	2.241

counterparts operated a mean of 34.117 acres. Total grain crops had a mean acreage of 1.827 for the Tubbercurry group and 0.627 for the Scarriff group. In each case, oats were predominant among the grain crops. Similarly, potatoes were pre-eminent among the root and green crops, of which the Tubbercurry operators had 0.620 acres and the Scarriff operators had 1.435 acres. Hay occupied about 6 acres on the Tubbercurry farms and about 9 acres on the Scarriff farms. However, in both cases, the bulk of the farm land was devoted to pasture, the amount being 21.767 acres for the Tubbercurry operators and 20.524 acres for the Scarriff operators.

b. Livestock

As might be expected from the high proportion of farm land devoted to pasture, cattle occupied a prominent place among the farm livestock enterprises. As shown in table 20, farm operator

TABLE 20. 1966 livestock enterprises of farm operator plant employees

Characteristic (mean)	Tubbercurry (n = 15)	Scarriff (n = 17)
Cows	4.2	4.7
Heifers-in-calf	1.7	1.3
Other cattle	11.6	13.5
Total cattle	17.5	19.5
Ewes	0.8	2.2
Other sheep	0.7	2.9
Total sheep	1.5	5.1
Sows	0.0	0.4
Other pigs	1.3	2.8
Total pigs	1.3	3.2
Turkeys, geese and ducks	2.7	6.4
Ordinary fowl	21.3	15.9
Total poultry	24.0	22.3

plant employees in Tubbercurry had a mean of 17.5 cattle, compared with 19.5 by the Scarriff farm operator plant employees. Approximately one fourth of the cattle were milch cows in each case.

Farm operator plant employees in Scarriff had a mean of about 5 sheep, considerably more than had the Tubbercurry group. Similarly, the Scarriff group had more pigs than had their Tubbercurry counterparts. There were but slight differences in numbers of poultry kept.

c. Labour use

Table 21 shows particulars regarding labour use on these farms. Farms operated by the farm operator plant employees in Tubbercurry had slightly more family members who did some work on those farms than had the corresponding farms in Scarriff. Operator time devoted to farm work was somewhat over 900 man-hours in each case. However, the number of man-hours of total family labour used in farming was about 400 higher on the Tubbercurry farms. This is consistent with the

TABLE 21. 1966 labour utilization on farms of farm operator plant employees

Characteristic (mean)	Tubbercurry (n = 15)	Scarriff (n = 17)
Number of family members doing some farm work	2.4	2.2
Man hours operator labour per annum	930.0	922.6
Total man hours family labour per annum	2,288.7	1,853.5
Number of days hired labour	33.1	16.5
Total man hours family plus hired labour per annum	2,553.7	1,985.7

presence of more other family members to work on these farms.

Farm operator plant employees employed more hired labour in Tubbercurry (33 days) than in Scarriff (16.5 days). Thus, the total number of man-hours of family plus hired labour used on the Tubbercurry farms was over 550 more than that used on the Scarriff farms.

d. Machinery

The mean estimated selling value of farm machinery and equipment on farms operated by farm operator plant employees was £57.3 in Tubbercurry and £43.2 in Scarriff. Many of these operators reported that whatever machinery and equipment they had was now obsolete and had no current selling value.

e. Farm income

Data pertaining to the current farm income of plant employee farm operators are shown in table 22. Farm operator plant employees in Scarriff reported mean sales of farm products amounting to £541, £183 more than reported by the Tubbercurry plant employee farm operators. The value of farm products consumed in their farm households was roughly similar

TABLE 22. 1966 farm income on farms of farm operator plant employees

Characteristic (mean)	Tubbercurry (n = 15)	Scarriff (n = 17)
	£	£
Total sales of farm products	358.3	541.1
Household consumption	86.0	80.1
Gross output	444.3	621.2
Non-labour expenses	213.5	310.4
Farm labour income	230.8	310.8
Hired labour expenses	41.0	15.8
Family farm income	189.8	295.0

for both groups of farm operators. Hence, the gross farm output of these farms was £621 in Scarriff and £444 in Tubbercurry.

However, farm operator plant employees had higher non-labour farm expenses in Scarriff than in Tubbercurry, so the labour income on those Scarriff farms was £311, compared with £231 on the Tubbercurry farms, a difference of £80. The Tubbercurry plant employee farm operators had used somewhat more hired labour, so their labour expenses were correspondingly higher than those of their Scarriff counterparts. Hence, family farm income was £295 on farms operated by plant employee farm operators in Scarriff, compared with £190 on the corresponding Tubbercurry farms, a difference of slightly over £100.

6

Hypothetical Industrialization Effects

The location of a new industrial plant in a predominantly rural community can be expected to have many social and economic effects. Some of these effects may be felt by households in the area. Other effects may be felt by business firms in the community —both farm business and non-farm business firms. The present study focused primarily on the economic impact of local industrialization on households and on farm businesses in two areas of Western Ireland. To a lesser extent, some of the effects on non-farm businesses were examined.

The economic effects of a newly established industrial plant on households and business firms in an area depend on the product demand and factor demand characteristics of the new plant.

In the two areas studied, it was expected that these effects would arise mainly from the factor demand characteristics of the new plants. This expectation arose from the fact that the markets for chipboard, locks and tooling products were practically entirely outside the two areas involved. Hence, sales of these products within the two areas would have little if any effect on production. In addition, cost reductions to local business firms selling these products in the two areas (arising from lower transportation charges or direct purchase from the factory) would be small, because sales of those products within the areas would be relatively insignificant. Furthermore, hardly any close complementarity or substitution relationships in production existed between these products and the products of other local firms.

The types of factors (inputs) demanded by a new industrial

firm depend on the type of product manufactured while the quantities which are demanded are closely related to the level of demand for the product manufactured. The new firms needed building facilities, machinery, assembly line equipment, office equipment and supplies, electricity, water and other utilities, transportation services and labour. In addition, the Tubbercurry firms required metal and metal products, while the Scarriff plant required timber, glue and some other factors. Demand for buildings, machines, office and assembly line equipment would be determined mainly by plant size and would be concentrated in the initial stages of the firms' operations. The demand for other inputs would be closely related to the level of production over time.

A. DIRECT AND INDIRECT EFFECTS

The effects of industrialization may be direct or indirect. Direct effects of industrialization are defined as those changes in household and business characteristics which are associated with the employment of particular factors of production at a newly established plant. The magnitude of these direct effects of the factor demand of a new firm on the local community depends on the ability of the community to supply these inputs to the new firm at prices competitive with sources of supply outside the community.

Since there were no other manufacturing firms in the two areas defined, the bulk of the non-labour inputs required by the new firms in these areas were likely to be obtained from wholesale firms outside these areas or by direct purchase from manufacturers located in other areas. Since the two areas were characterized by net emigration of population, the new firms would be expected to obtain a large proportion of the labour needed from within the two areas. Hence, the major direct effects of industrialization to be expected in these two areas would be those direct effects associated with the employment of labour in the new plants.

These direct effects would be those changes in household and business characteristics associated with the employment of a household member at one of the new plants. The direct effects of industrialization on local farm businesses are of special interest in the present study. An example of a direct effect on a farm business would be any reorganization of farming activity as a result of a farm operator having less time to spend at farm work following acceptance of factory employment.

Indirect effects of industrialization can also occur. Indirect effects of industrialization may be defined as those changes which industrialization induces in the external environment in which households and businesses function. These effects may alter the demand situation facing households and firms for the goods and services which they have to offer. On the other hand, these effects may also alter the supply situation of goods and services which households and business wish to acquire.

Examples of the first type of indirect effect would be any additional increased employment (affecting demand for labour sources from households) and income (affecting demand for products supplied by business firms) generated in the community via a multiplier following the direct effects. The second type of indirect effect may be illustrated by any reorganization of resources on farms using hired labour in the community arising from a rise in the level of farm wages caused by local industrial development.

B. SELECTIVITY ASPECTS OF INDUSTRIALIZATION EFFECTS

Productive factors hired or used by a new manufacturing plant are not likely to possess the same characteristics as those factors which are not hired or used by the new plant. To the extent that such differences occur, there is, therefore, a selectivity aspect involved in the incidence of the direct effects of industrialization on a community. Such selectivity can arise from the hiring policies of the new industrial firm or may arise from certain characteristics of some factors which result in those particular factors not being offered to the new firm for employment.

More specifically, one may expect that people who are em-

ployed at a newly established plant will differ in some respects
from other people within the area who are not so employed. The
nature of the selectivity involved depends largely on (a) the factors
motivating people to offer their labour services to the new firm
and (b) the nature of the newly created demands for labour
services. The importance of selectivity considerations may arise
as follows. It may be that an offer of labour services to the new
plant would be prompted by a desire to improve personal or
family position through increased income, higher occupational
status or better working conditions. If these selectivity aspects are
such that people who obtain employment at a new plant initially
have lower incomes than those who do not obtain such employment, then the direct effects of industrialization would, because
of these selectivity factors, tend to reduce income inequality in
the area of impact.

In particular, it is expected that newly created non-farm jobs
would attract some farm people into urban employment. Some
of these might be farm operators, the remainder being other
members of farm families. It is to be expected that farm people
who take non-farm jobs are not likely to be representative of all
farm people in the area. On a priori grounds, it is possible to
postulate certain farm and family circumstances which would
favour the obtaining of non-farm employment by members of
farm families.

One of the characteristics contributing to selectivity may be
family farm income. If family farm income is relatively low on
certain farms, and if there appear be few opportunities available
for increasing farm income, then operators and other family
members from these farms may seek non-farm employment as a
means of supplementing farm income.

When the desire for greater family income is the major motiva-
tion component, it follows that farm people who offer their labour
services to a newly established plant anticipate a net increase in
their incomes. This implies that the marginal return to their
labour is smaller in their farm businesses than in non-farm work.
The larger this differential, other things being equal, the greater

will be the pressure to find non-farm jobs. Thus, people who are experiencing a low marginal return to their labour are expected to offer their labour services for industrial employment more frequently than those who are experiencing a high marginal return.

Under given conditions regarding prices of farm products and costs of farm inputs, the marginal return to the labour of farm operators and other members of farm families is closely associated with the effective quantities of land and capital which are combined with this labour. Within certain limits, the more land and capital that are combined with labour, the greater the marginal return to labour may be expected to be. Hence, offers of labour services for non-farm employment may be expected to come most often from families on farms which have the smaller effective inputs of land and capital. The frequency of such offers may be expected to decrease as the effective inputs of land and capital increase.

If farm price conditions are favourable, people working on well-organized farms (in terms of the usual economic efficiency criteria) will earn returns to their labour which compare favourably to the wages offered in non-farm employment. However, if farm prices are unfavourable, labour returns, even on well-organized farms, will lie below those available in non-farm employment. Under such circumstances, some operators and other family members from farms with relatively large inputs of land and capital may offer their labour services for non-farm employment. However, the frequency of such offers is likely to be much lower than among families on farms with smaller inputs of land and capital. Hence, the generation of new non-farm employment opportunities in an area is likely to attract a larger proportion of farm people with low incomes and small amounts of land and capital than of those with high incomes and large amounts of land and capital.

In general, the labour demands of a newly established plant are likely to be specific in many cases. For some jobs, the new firm will desire to hire workers having certain characteristics, which some people will be better able to meet than others. If the firm is able to find people having the desired characteristics, those not possessing such characteristics will not be hired, even if they offer their services for employment. Hence, the hiring policies of the new firm partly determine the type of selectivity which characterizes industrialization.

Selectivity may be associated with age. Hiring policy of the new plant may favour the recruitment of younger workers, while older people may also be more vocationally immobile. The new firm may favour male employees over female employees. The firm may prefer to hire workers with previous non-farm work experience as opposed to those without such experience. Similarly, people with such prior non-farm work experience may more readily offer their labour services to the new firm. Subjective feelings regarding the desirability of certain characteristics of alternative employment opportunities may also influence the degree to which farm people offer their services to the new plant. To the extent that there are selectivity aspects involved, both arising from the hiring policies of the new firms and from other family or personal characteristics, the people who obtain employment at the new plant are likely to differ with respect to some attributes from those who do not obtain such employment.

C. EMPLOYMENT AND WAGE EFFECTS

The demand for labour by the new industrial plants would theoretically shift the aggregate demand schedule for labour in both areas to the right as depicted in figure 4. It should be understood that this increase in demand for labour services would be relative to the demand for labour services which would have existed in those areas in the absence of the new manufacturing plants, not relative to the demand for labour services which existed in those areas at the time when the new industrial plants commenced operations.

For a given increase in demand for labour services, the effects on employment and wage rates in an area depend on the aggre-

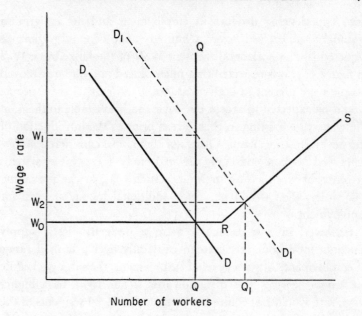

Figure 4.   Effect of increased demand for labour services on employment
and wage rates

gate supply schedule for labour services in the area. The shape of this schedule was not known in either area. It was theoretically possible that this schedule was perfectly inelastic in both areas as shown by the line QQ in figure 4. With such a supply schedule, an increase in the demand for labour services from DD to D_1D_1 would result in an increase in the wage rate from W_0 to W_1, with the level of employment remaining unchanged. It was decided to reject this possibility for both areas, since both areas had been characterized by declining employment and by net emigration during the period prior to the establishment of the new industrial plants. It was also decided that a supply schedule for labour services which sloped upwards to the left was unrealistic for both areas, since the areas had relatively low levels of income per capita.

It was felt, on the other hand, that it was reasonable to expect that the supply schedule for labour services in areas which had been experiencing declines in employment and net emigration would be quite elastic over a limited range of employment, as depicted by the horizontal segment W_0R of the kinked line W_0S in figure 4. It was expected that unemployed and *under*employed people were present in both areas. Some, at least, of these people would be expected to accept employment, if available to them, at the wage rate existing in those areas prior to the introduction of the new industrial plants. Others of them, also considered *under*-employed as conventionally defined, may have value systems in terms of work-leisure preference such that, at the prevailing wage rate, they would not offer additional labour services for employment.

However, in any particular area, a perfectly elastic supply schedule for labour services can exist only over a limited range of employment. At some level of employment, the supply schedule for labour services will turn upwards to the right, as a higher wage rate would be required to attract additional residents of the areas into the labour force or to induce workers from outside the areas to accept employment at the new plants. In figure 4, such a situation is depicted by the upward sloping segment RS of the line W_0S which is the supply curve for labour services intersecting with D_1D_1 the new demand curve for labour services, giving an employment level of Q_1 at a wage rate of W_2, as compared with the initial employment level of Q at a wage rate of W_0.

The aggregate labour market in an area is more likely to consist of a number of separate markets for different types of labour services than to be a single labour market. It will suffice for purposes of the present discussion to view the labour markets in the two areas of interest as consisting of a market for unskilled labour services and a market for skilled labour services. Training of workers and the introduction of an apprenticeship program at one of the Tubbercurry plants indicated that the supply schedule for certain types of labour services demanded at that plant was less than perfectly elastic in the area.

Training of workers at the plant would shift the supply schedule for skilled labour services to the right as shown in figure 5A, which represents a market for skilled labour services. Depending

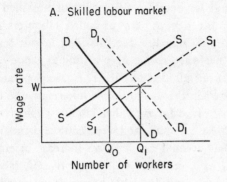

A. Skilled labour market

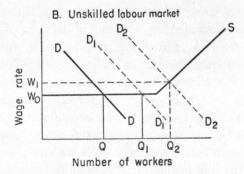

B. Unskilled labour market

Figure 5.   Effects of increased demand for labour services on labour and wage rates in skilled and unskilled labour markets

on the amount of increase in the supply schedule relative to the increase in the demand schedule, the wage rate for skilled labour would increase, decrease, or remain unchanged as depicted in figure 5A. It was expected that the wage rate for skilled labour in the Tubbercurry area would not decline, since skilled labour would be likely to migrate from the area if the skilled wage rate declined. However, the increase in the supply schedule may have been sufficient to keep the skilled wage rate unchanged in the area.

The demand schedule for unskilled labour services would shift to the right, as depicted in figure 5B, either as a result of the increased demand for actual employment of unskilled labourers at the plant or the demand for unskilled labourers for future training. The supply schedule for unskilled labour services was expected to be perfectly elastic over a limited range of employment for the reasons alluded to earlier. Again depending on the amount of increase in the demand schedule relative to the supply schedule the wage rate for unskilled labour would remain constant or increase. In figure 5B, an increase in the demand schedule from DD to D_1D_1 would result in an increase in employment from Q_0 to Q_1 at a constant wage rate W_0. If, however, the demand schedule for unskilled labour services increased to D_2D_2, then the level of employment would be at Q_2, while the wage rate would have risen to W_1.

From the foregoing analysis, it was expected that employment in both areas would increase as a result of the demand for labour services by the new industrial plants. However, the probable effects on wage rates are not as evident. Any upgrading of the levels of skill of the labour force in these areas would tend to raise average wage rates, while wage rates for various types of labour services would either increase or remain constant. Since the new factories in both areas were a major source of employment in the towns wherein situated, the most probable effect was that the increases in demand for labour services by the new plants would lead to increases in average wage rates in both areas.

Hypotheses can also be developed regarding the geographical incidence of the employment effects of a new industrial plant. In any particular occupation and in any specific grade of skill within that occupation, the employees of the new plant may be expected to receive a wage rate which is unrelated to the distance travelled to and from work by those employees. Such commuting involves transportation costs and loss of leisure time, both of which are roughly proportional to distance travelled. Because of these costs of commuting, the proportion of population and the actual number of workers commuting to work at the new industrial plants were expected to be inversely related to distance from the plants, due to the decreasing net differential between wages received and total cost of commuting. Indirect wage adjustments in both areas would therefore be expected to diminish with increasing distance from the new plants.

Increases in population and incomes per capita usually arise from increases in employment and wage rates. These increases would then be expected to lead to an increase in the demand for goods and services sold by other firms in these areas. This, in turn, might lead to an increase in demand for labour services by those other business firms. This indirect employment effect would probably be quite small relative to the direct employment effect in both areas studied, since it is reasonable to expect that in areas experiencing declining employment and net emigration some business firms have unused capacity. However, any indirect employment effects which would occur in those areas would generate additional upward pressure on wage rates in both areas.

D.   POPULATION EFFECTS

Although increases in employment are usually accompanied by increases in population, an increase in employment in an area can occur without an increase in an area's population. Employment of persons residing within the area who were formerly unemployed, employment of persons residing within the area who were formerly employed outside the area or employment of persons who commute from outside the area would give rise to an increase in employment within the area but not to an increase in the population of the area.

It was likely, however, since the new industrial plants would have a relatively large employment in both areas, that population as well as employment would rise in both areas. Here again, it must be borne in mind that an increase is to be understood as an increase in population relative to what population would have been in the absence of the new plants, not relative to what population was prior to the establishment of the new plants. Persons who remained in these areas as a result of obtaining employment following the establishment of the new industrial plants and who would otherwise have emigrated from these areas would increase these areas' population. Similarly, any migration of workers into the areas would increase population. Since some of these workers would be heads of households, population would be expected to increase by some multiple of the number of employees in these two categories.

In was also expected that such increases in population would be greater in and around Scarriff and Tubbercurry than in other parts of the two areas, since, as hypothesized earlier, increases in employment at the new plants would be greater in and around Scarriff and Tubbercurry than in other parts of the two areas. In addition, persons and families who migrated to the two areas as a result of employment at the two plants would be likely to reside in and around Scarriff and Tubbercurry in proximity to their new places of employment.

It is therefore hypothesized that population increased in the two areas as a result of the new industrial activity and that this increase in population diminished accordingly as distance from the new manufacturing plants increased.

E.   INCOME EFFECTS

Even if wage rates in both areas remained constant, total and per capita income would be expected to increase. Any increase in the number of employed workers from within the areas would raise total income, assuming no decrease in hours worked by each employee. Employment at the prevailing wage rate of previously unemployed workers residing within the areas would increase income per capita as well as total income. *Under*employed persons in the areas might be expected to accept employment at the new plants if they expected an increase in income as a result. For example, operators of smaller farms and small local businesses might expect to increase their incomes by accepting employment at the new plants while continuing to operate their farms and. businesses. Lastly, any upgrading of labour associated with training of workers at the new plants, or migration to the areas of more highly skilled employees, would increase total income and income per capita in the areas even though wage rates remained constant.

Any increase in wage rates in the two areas would give rise to additional increases in total income and income per capita, unless a corresponding decrease occurred in the number of hours worked. However, it was expected that hours worked per employee would remain constant or increase, since the new industrial plants would increase the aggregate demand for labour services in the two areas. Since wage rate adjustments would be expected to decrease with distance from the industrial plants, any increases in income per capita in the areas due to increases in wage rates would also be expected to decrease with distance from Scarriff and Tubbercurry.

Increases in total income and income per capita within the two areas would be expected to occur. These increases would also be expected to be greater in and around Scarriff and Tubbercurry than in other parts of the two areas, since employment and population were expected to increase more in the parts of the areas closest to Scarriff and Tubbercurry.

F.   HOUSEHOLD EXPENDITURE EFFECTS

Aggregate demand for goods and services sold by business firms in the two areas would be expected to increase as a result of increased consumer expenditures arising from the increases in population and income. It is well to remember once more that this increase in demand must be considered relative to the level of demand in these areas in the absence of the new plants, not to the level of demand in the period just prior to the commencement of industrial activity. An increase in population and/or income per capita would increase the demand schedule facing business firms selling various types of consumer goods and services.

However, it was also expected that some employees who lived in the outlying parts of the two areas would shift their shopping patterns in favour of Scarriff and Tubbercurry. In addition, since the increase in population would be greatest in and around these towns, the incidence of the expenditure effects could also be expected to be greatest in and around Scarriff and Tubbercurry.

G.   FARM BUSINESS EFFECTS

1. Direct effects

Direct effects of industrialization on farm businesses are those changes in farming activity which result on farms from which the farm operator or another member of the farm family accepted employment at the new industrial plant. In the present study, major attention is focused on the direct effects on farm businesses which arise as a result of farm operators accepting industrial employment.

Industrial employment of a farm operator may affect his farm business by increasing the relative scarcity of operator labour and also by stimulating farm investment. If a desire for increased income induces a farm operator to take a non-farm job, it is reasonable to infer from this that the marginal return to his labour is greater in the non-farm job than in his farm business. Hence, the opportunity cost of non-farm labour may increase with non-farm employment. Depending on the elasticity of supply of operator labour with respect to income, this increased opportunity cost may induce adjustments in farm inputs, in product mix, in farm output and in farm income.

On the other hand, an increase in the income of a farm family associated with non-farm employment may give rise to an increase in family savings and lead to a reduction in the opportunity cost of investing in the farm business. Such a reduction in the opportunity cost of farm investment may induce farm capital formation and increased use of more productive reproducible farm inputs. This income effect may, to a certain extent, counteract any adjustment pressures in the farm business which arise because of a reduction in availability of operator labour. While bearing this possibility in mind, some of the direct effects of industrialization on farm business are examined hereunder in more detail.

a.   Labour use

The employment of a farm operator at an industrial plant may or may not reduce the labour input in his farm business, depending on various possible substitution effects.

One possibility may be that prior to industrial employment the farm operator was engaged in farm duties for only a small proportion of his total available time. This might be expected to occur if the effective quantities of land and capital on his farm were extremely small, so that the marginal return to his labour in his farm business would be so low that he would devote a high proportion of his time to leisure. Under such circumstances, availability of industrial employment at a considerably higher rate of return to his labour might result in a large substitution of income-generating activity for leisure. In accepting industrial employment, he may merely utilize his available time more fully without decreasing the amount of time devoted to farm work.

In general, however, industrial employment involves a large and relatively constant input of time on the part of industrial employees. In general, also, the amount of time devoted by farm operators to strictly leisure activities is less than the amount of time usually required as an input in industrial employment. It may well be that an operator has been devoting a large amount of time to farm work, but that his labour has not been very productive, due to the low levels of other inputs available to him. Industrial employment of such an operator would be expected to induce a substitution of industrial work for leisure and a substitution of industrial work for farm work. His time devoted to farm work would decline, but such decline would be less than the time devoted to industrial employment, because of an increase in total time worked.

In a third situation, industrial employment of a farm operator may result in a decline in his time spent at farm work roughly equal to the time devoted to his industrial employment. Such a situation would arise when the operator's total work time was already large. Industrial employment would then involve a substitution of one work activity (industrial work) for another (farm work). It was felt that most farm operators in both areas fell in the second or third category described. Hence, it was expected that some reduction in time devoted to farm work would occur in the case of most farm operators accepting employment at the new plants.

The direct effects of industrial employment of a farm operator on his farm business are strongly influenced by the labour situation on his farm. Even when the time spent at farm work by the farm operator declines as a result of his industrial employment, it need not follow that a reduction in total labour used on his farm will occur, as other farm labour (either family or hired) may be available to substitute for that lost to industrial employment.

The extent to which family labour may be substituted for operator labour is influenced by family size and composition, which determine the availability of potential substitute labour on a farm. The extent to which this potential substitute labour is utilized to substitute for operator labour depends on the rate at which these people can transform some of their present activities into the equivalent of operator labour and also on their desire to do so.

Considerable variability was expected in these characteristics among farm families. This would give rise to wide variation among farms in the amount of labour substitution for a given loss of operator labour. However, it was expected that some increase in amount of time devoted to farm work by other family members was likely to occur on most farms the operators of which had accepted industrial employment.

b. Farm investment

In general, industrial employment of a farm operator may be expected to increase the total income of a farm family. This may give rise to an increase in family savings, which, in turn, would tend to reduce the opportunity cost of investment in the farm business. The influence of this effect would be present even on farms where family labour substituted completely for any operator labour lost through industrial employment.

However, the increased opportunity cost of operator labour to the farm business may induce efforts to economize on the use of labour. This, coupled with a decreased opportunity cost of farm investment funds, may result in an increase in the use of labour-saving machinery and methods. This would be most likely to occur when family labour cannot be substituted readily for operator labour, because of its low elasticity of supply on some farms. Such an adjustment might take the form of acquisition of machinery and equipment or its hiring.

Apart from investment induced by labour-saving, a decrease in the opportunity cost of farm investment funds may give rise to increased investment in new and improved reproducible farm inputs. Increases may occur in expenditures on such inputs as better seeds and fertilizers, more or improved livestock, etc. Investment may take place to increase the effective input of land on a farm, either by purchasing or renting additional land or by improving the productivity of existing land on the farm through drainage or other reclamation processes.

c. Cropping pattern

Industrial employment of a farm operator may give rise to adjustments in land utilization. However, as noted earlier, the effect of greater scarcity of operator labour may be partly off-set by the investment effects arising from increased family income.

An increase in the scarcity of operator labour may be expected to induce a substitution of labour-extensive crops for labour-intensive crops. In particular, it may be expected that in the areas studied a reduction would occur in the acreage under potatoes and other root crops along with a reduction in acreage under grain crops on farms, the operators of which accepted industrial employment. This would be accompanied by a cor-responding increase in acreage under hay and pasture, except to the extent that a reduction in total acreage farmed was involved.

There may be a reduction in total acreage farmed, especially if crops, the acreage under which is being reduced, were grown on land rented on a conacre system. On the other hand, as already noted, the investment effect may induce an increase in acreage farmed. Hence, the most probable net effect on total acreage farmed depends on the relative strength of these two effects.

Pressure for adjustments in cropping patterns may be expected to be greatest on farms where a substantial increase occurred in the opportunity cost of operator labour, where the supply of other farm labour is highly inelastic and where the reduction in the opportunity cost of farm investment funds was slight. Such adjustment pressure would be least (or possibly non-existent) on farms characterized by the negation of the foregoing attributes.

d. Livestock pattern

Similar effects may be expected in the case of livestock enterprises on farms the operator of which has accepted industrial employment. An increase in the scarcity of operator labour would induce a reduction in labour-intensive livestock enterprises and a possible increase in labour-extensive livestock enterprises, though not necessarily requiring the latter.

In particular, in the study areas, it was expected that industrial employment of farm operators would induce a decline in numbers of pigs and dairy cows kept and an increase in the number of other (dry) cattle. However, the reduction in number of dairy cows might be counteracted on some farms by the investment effect, especially if the supply of other farm labour on these farms were fairly elastic.

It was expected that a shift from labour-intensive to labour-extensive enterprises would occur both in terms of cropping and livestock patterns since the most frequently adopted labour-extensive livestock enterprise in those areas (rearing of beef cattle) is highly complementary with the most frequently adopted labour-extensive crop (pasture) in the study areas.

e. Farm output and farm income

Obviously, the impact which industrial employment of a farm operator will have on the output of his farm depends on the magnitude of the substitution effects (both factor and product) and on the magnitude and kind of net investment effects on the farm business. Circumstances under which a decrease in farm output would be most likely to occur may be described as follows : low income elasticity of supply of operator and family labour, lack of opportunity to effect labour economies in crop and/or livestock production and a low propensity to invest in the farm business.

These circumstances are not as likely to be characteristic of farms where operators have accepted industrial employment as frequently as they are characteristic of other farms. The operator of a farm where such circumstances prevail would have considerably less incentive to seek non-farm employment, other things being equal, than would operators of farms not so circumstanced. Selectivity aspects, therefore, are expected to be of importance in influencing the incidence of industrial employment among farm operators in such a manner that their industrial employment would not be expected to reduce farm output on most of the farms involved.

Maintenance of farm output at its level prior to the acceptance of industrial employment might be accomplished in one or more of several ways. The farm operator may work harder while at farm work, he may rise earlier or work later into evening-time or he may allocate his time more effectively. The operator's wife or other family members may compensate for the loss in operator labour. Greater recourse may be had to labour-saving technology; while the investment effect arising from increased total family income would also tend to boost farm output.

Arising from the foregoing, it would also be expected that industrial employment in both areas involved but slight, if any, reductions in farm income. Where farm output declined as a result of industrial employment, it would be expected that farm income would decline also. However, since the decreases in output were expected to be slight, any decreases in farm income were also expected to be slight. It would, therefore, appear that most of the additional income obtained by farm families as a result of industrial employment of farm operators would represent a net increase to the total family income of such farm families in both areas.

2. Indirect effects

Indirect effects on farm businesses may arise as a result of local industrialization. These may involve changes in the supply situation for farm inputs or the demand situation for farm products. An indirect effect of the first type might arise if the increased demand for labour services by the new industrial plant led to an increase in the local level of wage rates, including wages paid to hired farm labour. Such an increase might be expected to induce adjustments in resources, output and income on farms which use moderate to substantial amounts of hired labour. However, in the two study areas, the quantity of hired labour used on most farms is negligible; hence this effect was not expected to be of high magnitude.

The second type of indirect effect might be expected to occur following an increase in an area's population or income per capita. If a new industrial plant gives rise to a direct population increase, this, in turn, would be expected to shift the demand schedule for farm products within that area. An indirect effect of increased income on consumption might also occur following employment of workers at a new plant. This might also lead to an increased demand for some farm products. However, the income elasticity of demand for most farm products would appear to be relatively low. Hence, increases in an area's income per capita would not be likely to generate much of an increased demand for farm products.

In addition, it is also possible that any increased demand for farm products might be met by farm producers outside the area involved. This "leakage" would reduce the indirect effect on farm businesses in the area itself. It either case, the incidence of these indirect effects would be quite diffuse and their magnitude difficult to quantify. In the present study, no rigorous attempt was made to estimate the magnitude of these indirect effects.

3. Selectivity aspects

The concept of selectivity has been discussed in detail earlier in the present chapter. The decision of a farm operator to seek employment at a newly established industrial plant may be presumed to result after careful consideration on his part. It is to be expected that such a decision would be influenced to a large extent by family and farm characteristics. Whether or not he might actually obtain such employment, given his decision to seek it, may, in turn, be influenced by the hiring policy of the new firm. For these reasons, therefore, it was expected that, in both areas, it should be possible to discern certain differences in personal and farm characteristics between farm operators who obtained employment at the new plant and those who did not obtain such employment.

The farm differences would be expected to be manifested in such characteristics as farm income, farm size, value of farm machinery, quantities of livestock, etc. The personal differences would be expected to be associated with age, education, previous non-farm work experience, etc.

H. SUMMARY OF HYPOTHESES

The hypotheses in the present study regarding the impact of the establishment of new industrial plants at Scarriff and Tubbercurry on the surrounding areas are summarized hereunder. Survey data collected in the course of the present study will be used to evaluate these hypotheses.

(1) The new plants directly increased employment in the two areas. This increase consisted of people who were newly drawn into the labour force, people from outside these

areas who moved into the areas and people who would have left the areas in the absence of obtaining employment at the new plants. The employment effect diminished as distance from Scarriff and Tubbercurry increased.

(2) Population in both areas increased, due to immigration of some workers and their families and the non-emigration from the areas of some workers and their families who would otherwise have left the areas. The population effect diminished as distance from Scarriff and Tubbercurry increased.

(3) Incomes in both areas increased. The increase in total income and in income per household diminished as distance from Scarriff and Tubbercurry increased.

(4) Increased incomes of employee households resulted in increased expenditures on goods and services. There was also a shift in the incidence of purchases of goods and services from the outlying parts of the two areas in favour of purchases in the towns of Scarriff and Tubbercurry.

(5) Acceptance of industrial employment by farm operators resulted in resource adjustments and product mix adjustments on their farms.

(6) The most frequently occurring resource adjustment on such farms was labour substitution.

(7) Decreases in total farm output were not necessitated on most farms the operators of which accepted industrial employment.

(8) Farm and personal characteristics differentiated the farm operators who obtained industrial employment from those who did not obtain such employment.

7

Methodological Considerations

The methodological considerations involved in the identification and measurement of industrialization effects in Western Ireland are discussed in this chapter. Section A contains a general discussion regarding problems involved in measurement of the effects. The selection and delineation of the study areas is discussed in section B. The sources of data used in the study are detailed in section C. Section D describes the manner in which the direct effects of industrialization were estimated, while section E contains a discussion of the methods used in the examination of the selectivity factors involved.

A. PROBLEMS OF MEASUREMENT

Difficult problems arise in attempting to identify and measure the effects of industrialization. One of these is the problem of accurately measuring the changes in the variables studied. Measurement of change implies the availability of data pertaining to at least two points in time. Changes in primary data can be measured most accurately if the desired information is collected at each relevant point in time, as such a procedure tends to minimize memory bias.

Ideally, measurement of changes induced by industrialization would require a benchmark study in an area prior to the introduction of the new industrial plant the impact of which it is desired to study. This benchmark study would be followed at a later date by one or more studies undertaken after the new plant had been in operation.

Accurate measurement of change in the relevant variables, however, is not the most difficult problem encountered. After a new industrial plant has been established in an area, other forces which may generate changes in the variables being studied continue to operate. Hence, the measured changes in these variables may reflect the result of industrialization or of other forces. More likely, they will reflect a combination of effects emanating from the industrialization and from other forces which may generate change. Thus, there is the problem of determining how much, if any, of the observed changes in the relevant variables can be attributed to the effects of industrialization and how much to the effects of other forces.

One approach to the solution of this latter problem would involve undertaking a controlled experiment type of study. In such a study, in addition to the area wherein the new industrial plant had been located, one or more control areas would be selected on the basis of over-all similarity to the area of interest. The only significant difference among these areas during the study period would be that the area of interest would have experienced industrialization, while the other(s) would not.

The variables of interest would be measured during the base period and during or at the end of the study period. Changes occurring in these variables in the area of interest and in the control area(s) would then be calculated and the difference between these changes would be attributed to the effect of industrialization.

Some variables which might be examined in such a study would be total area employment, sectoral employment, total income, income per capita, manufacturing output, manufacturing sales, retail sales, agricultural output, local taxation base, income tax payments, population, age distribution of population, net migration into or out of the area, educational expansion, etc.

A study of the foregoing nature would be suited to the identification of the *total* effects of industrialization, i.e. the combined direct and indirect effects, which have been discussed in the previous chapter. It would not be possible to separate these effects, nor to estimate the nature and magnitude of the selectivity aspects involved.

An alternative approach involves a survey type study. Such a study provides the best approach for observing the direct effects of industrialization and the influence of the selectivity factors.

Ideally, in order to measure the selectivity factors, it would be desirable to have prior to their acceptance of plant employment, data regarding the personal, household and farm business characteristics of those people who obtained plant employment. Such data could be compared with data pertaining to the same time period regarding the same characteristics of those people who did not obtain plant employment. From this comparison, the nature and magnitude of the selectivity factors could be estimated.

The original data regarding the personal, household and farm business characteristics of those people who accepted plant employment could subsequently be compared with data regarding the same characteristics of these people during or at the end of the study period. Thus, combined direct and indirect effects of industrialization might be elucidated. Groups of people could be identified who in the base period had attributes similar to those of the people who obtained plant employment, except that these groups did not obtain plant employment. Changes occurring during the study period in the personal, household and farm business characteristics of these groups could be measured. Differences between the changes observed in the characteristics of the plant employee group and the changes observed in the characteristics of groups possessing initially similar attributes would be due to the direct effects of industrialization.

Since the plants in both areas had been in operation for some few years prior to the present study being conceived, it was not possible to conduct a benchmark study. Because of the limitations on the availability of aggregate data pertaining to the areas of interest and because of the specific interest of the present study in the direct industrialization effects and in the selectivity factors, it was decided to conduct a survey type study in the two areas.

Towards this end, it was decided to interview all plant employees in both areas. In addition, a sample of heads of urban households which contained no plant employees and a sample of farm operators who were not employed at the plant were interviewed in each area.

The direct effects of industrialization were identified by direct questioning of plant employee respondents regarding changes arising as a result of their obtaining employment at the new plants. The magnitude of the selectivity factors was estimated indirectly by comparing characteristics of certain groups of plant employees with those of corresponding groups of other people from the area who did not obtain plant employment, after allowing for the direct effects reported by the plant employees.

This approach has two limitations. The first involves the ability of respondents to recall the direction and magnitude of changes in the relevant variables. The second involves their ability to identify portions of these changes as arising out of their obtaining plant employment. These limitations notwithstanding, it was felt that this approach provided the best available analytic framework for analysing the problem at hand and that it would provide interesting and useful results.

B.   SELECTION AND DELINEATION OF AREAS

The criteria used in selecting the study areas have been discussed earlier. Likewise, the manner in which the boundaries to those areas were determined has also been discussed.

At this point, however, it is appropriate to note that the area delineated around Tubbercurry contained the residences of 153 or 97.5 per cent of the 157 employees interviewed. 2 of the 4 who resided outside the area were residents of the town of Sligo. One resided near Ballysodare and one near Collooney.

The area delineated around Scarriff contained the residences of 137 or 90.7 per cent of the 151 plant employees who were interviewed. 13 of the 14 people who resided outside the area were residents of Co. Tipperary, hence being excluded, by definition, from the area, since they resided outside the undeveloped areas. Nearly all of these 13 plant employees resided in and around Ballina, Co. Tipperary, which as noted earlier is connected to Killaloe by a bridge across the River Shannon. The other employee who resided outside the area resided about 4 or 5 miles west of Tulla, Co. Clare.

C. SOURCES OF DATA

The field work in connection with the present study was conducted in the two areas during the summer of 1966. This section describes the manner in which the field work was organized and conducted and the types of data collected.

1. Plant employees

A complete listing of all employees was provided by the plant management personnel in each area. Facilities were kindly made available by the plant management personnel to enable the plant employees to be interviewed at the plants. Interviews were arranged with all plant employees up to and including the rank of working foreman. Clerical and secretarial personnel were included, but the management personnel were not included in the group to be interviewed.

There were 183 plant employees in Tubbercurry. 157 complete interviews were obtained. 4 of the employees were ill and thus not at work; 3 more were on holidays while the interviews were being conducted. 19 plant employees refused to cooperate in the study.

The Scarriff plant had 194 employees when the survey was conducted. 151 complete interviews were obtained. 3 plant employees were absent from work due to illness; 7 were on holidays, while there were 8 refusals. In addition there were 15 timber workers and 10 lorry drivers who were not available for interview. The latter have a brief turn-about period at the plant.

Data presented earlier regarding the sex distribution of all plant employees and of those plant employees interviewed was about the same as the proportion of males and females among the population of plant employees in each area.

Some differences may exist in Scarriff between the timber workers and lorry drivers on the one hand and the remainder of the plant employees on the other. However, a few of these workers were interviewed. Data regarding age, education, residence, income, etc., for these few employees did not differ appreciably from corresponding data pertaining to other plant employees. However, there were only a few cases involved. Hence, some caution may be advisable in generalizing from the results of the interviews with the other plant employees, because of the non-availability of most of the timber workers and lorry drivers for interview.

Two questionnaires were used in interviewing plant employees.[1] The first questionnaire was administered to all plant employees. Information was obtained regarding personal characteristics (age, sex, education, etc.) of the employee and the other members of his household, the employee's residential and occupational history since 1956, job attitude, length of time in plant employment, present earnings, previous earnings, estimated alternative local earnings in the absence of the plant, etc. Information was also obtained regarding the magnitude of any increases in household income reported as a result of obtaining plant employment, on the expenditure of these increased incomes and on shifts in shopping patterns induced as a result of obtaining plant employment.

In addition, the farm work association of each plant employee was determined during the course of the interview. An additional questionnaire was administered to each plant employee who was a farm operator. This farm questionnaire was designed to elicit information regarding land utilization, numbers of livestock, labour and machinery use and farm income. In addition, information was collected from those farm operators regarding the changes in their farm businesses which they made as a direct result of obtaining plant employment. The content of these

[1] Copies of the questionnaires may be obtained from the authors on request.

questionnaires will be referred to in more detail in the next section during the discussion of the methods used in estimating the direct effects of industrialization.

2. Farm operator sample

In order to determine the nature and magnitude of the selectivity factors affecting farm operator employment at the plants, a sample of farm operators who were not employed at the plants was drawn in each area. No list of farm operators was available, so the samples had to be drawn by indirect means which are outlined hereunder.

Irish agricultural statistics are collected in relation to "agricultural holdings". An "agricultural holding" is viewed as all land used wholly or partly for agricultural or livestock production that is operated, directed or managed by one person (the holder), alone or with the assistance of others, without regard to title, size or location, and may be in one or more pieces if they are in the same neighbourhood and are known and operated as a single holding or property. A lower limit of one quarter of an acre is adopted in the application of this criterion.

The enumeration districts are the District Electoral Divisions (DEDs). In the 1965 agricultural enumeration, where a holding lay partly in one DED and partly in one or more other DEDs, data pertaining to each part were enumerated separately in the DED in which that part of the holding was located. Hence, the number of holdings reported in each DED consisted of all holdings lying wholly or partly in that DED.

Such holdings, lying partly in two or more DEDs are referred to as "divided holdings". Adjustments in numbers of holdings to take account of the number of "divided holdings" are not published at the DED level. Such adjustments are made at the level of Rural Districts (sub-county aggregations of DEDs) and at higher levels of aggregation.

However, in respect of each holding, one specific point called the headquarters (usually where the farmyard is located) has been defined. When parts of a holding lie in two or more DEDs, it is possible to identify the DED in which the headquarters is situated.

It was decided, for the purposes of the present study, to confine attention to farms of five or more acres in extent. A sample of about 100 operators of such farms was desired in each area. An initial sampling fraction to provide this number of holdings (unadjusted for "divided holdings") was calculated. This sampling fraction was then increased by the ratio of the total number of holdings (including "divided holdings") to the number of whole holdings in the Rural District which comprised the bulk of each area.

A further adjustment was made to allow for non-interviews and for the possibility that some holdings as defined were no longer being operated as separate farms. These two adjustments resulted in a one-in-fourteen sampling fraction in the Scarriff area and a one-in-thirty sampling fraction in the Tubbercurry area. The Tubbercurry area had a larger number of holdings than had the Scarriff area, partly because the area was larger and partly because the holdings in the Tubbercurry area tended to be smaller than those in the Scarriff area.

In order to obtain representation in the sample from each DED, it was decided to stratify holdings by DED and to draw holdings at random within each DED, using the same sampling fraction for all DEDs in each area. A "headquarters rule" was devised for use in the case of "divided holdings". In the case of each "divided holding", such a holding was included in the sample if its headquarters lay in the DED for which that holding was drawn; such a holding was excluded if its headquarters lay in another DED. Thus every holding had an equal and independent chance of being drawn in the sample.

The number of agricultural holdings returned in the agricultural enumeration was expected to exceed the number of farm operators, for a variety of reasons. First of all, land let to other persons is not included as part of the holding of him to whom it has been let. Rather, it is included in the holding to which it had formerly belonged. Since whole holdings are sometimes let, the "holder" of such a holding would not be a farm operator and that holding would be operated by the renter either as a separate farm or, more likely, as part of and in conjunction with other land which he already was operating.

Secondly, other holdings which have ceased to be operated as farms may still be included as separate holdings for enumeration purposes. Examples of such holdings would be holdings which have been sold and are now being operated by other farmers as part of their farms, holdings sold to or acquired by the Irish Land Commission for redistribution to relieve land congestion, but which have not yet been reallocated, holdings sold to the Forestry Division of the Department of Lands for afforestation purposes, but which have not yet been planted and holdings whose owners may be elderly or unable to work and which are being operated by locally resident relatives of the owners in conjunction with their own farms.

The procedure used in deriving a sample of farm operators from the sample of holdings was as follows. All holdings in the sample which had been acquired by the Irish Land Commission or by the Department of Lands were identified. These had ceased to be operated as separate farms and were eliminated. Holdings in the sample which had been sold or let were identified. Where such a holding was being operated as a separate farm by the new owner or renter, the new owner or renter was interviewed and data collected pertaining to that farm. Where such a holding was being operated as part of another farm, it was eliminated. Similarly, in cases where the prospective interviewee had died since the lists of holdings had been revised the holding was included in the sample if it was currently being operated as a separate farm. If not, it was eliminated. Any farm operator plant employees who were drawn in the samples were eliminated therefrom, so that the sample would be representative of farm operators in both areas who had not obtained employment at the new plant.

For example, use of a one-in-fourteen sampling fraction in the Scarriff area and the application of the "headquarters rule" resulted in a sample of 120 holdings. 19 of these holdings had

ceased to be operated as separate farms, leaving 101 farm operators identified in the sample. One farm operator in the sample
had been interviewed at the Scarriff plant, leaving 100 eligible
farm operators. 79 complete interviews were obtained; there were
2 refusals and 19 farm operators were unobtainable for interview
by reason of illness, absence on vacation, not being at home on
repeated calls, etc.

Conventional stratified sampling techniques were used in
analysing the data obtained from the farm operator sample in the
Scarriff area regarding personal, household and farm business
characteristics.

Even when using a one-in-thirty sampling fraction in the
Tubbercurry area, 164 holdings resulted in the sample. As the
study progressed, time and other resources limited the collection
of the survey data. Subsequently, interviewing was confined to
22 of the 30 DEDs in the Tubbercurry area. These had a total of
128 holdings listed in the sample. Twenty-one holdings had
ceased to be operated as separate farms since the listings of
holdings had last been revised. Three farm operators in the sample
were plant employees, who had been interviewed in the plant.
Thus, there were 104 eligible farm operators. Complete interviews were obtained in respect of 80 of those, while the remaining
24 were unobtainable for similar reasons to those cited earlier
regarding the Scarriff rural sample.

Data obtained in these interviews were analysed using cluster
sampling techniques, the DEDs being treated as clusters.

3. Urban household sample

A stratified random sample of urban households was drawn in
each area, the towns in each area being treated as strata. A one-
in-five sample was drawn in the Scarriff area and a one-in-six
sample was drawn in the Tubbercurry area.

Urban households which contained plant employees were
eliminated from the samples. Urban households in which farm
operators resided were also eliminated, as such farm operators
had a chance to enter the farm operator sample.

Thus the urban household sample represents non-farm urban households containing no plant employees. Interviews were obtained with heads of the remaining households in the samples. Use was made of selected portions of the first questionnaire which had been administered to all plant employees.

77 complete interviews with heads of urban households were obtained in the Scarriff area and 72 complete interviews were obtained in the Tubbercurry area. Data obtained in these interviews were analysed by the use of conventional stratified sampling techniques.

D. ESTIMATION OF DIRECT EFFECTS

1. Employment

Several facets of the employment opportunities generated by the establishment of the new plants in Tubbercurry and in Scarriff were of interest. The extent to which the new plants drew some of their employees into the non-farm labour force for the first time was determined from the employment history of the plant employees as reported when they were interviewed. The extent of employee mobility into the areas from jobs located elsewhere was determined from an examination of the location of the previous employments of those plant employees who had been previously engaged in non-farm employment.

The major interest of the present study regarding employment lay in measuring the employment effects of the new plants. The true employment effect of a plant on an area at any given point in time is the difference between the actual level of employment in the area at that point in time and the level at which employment in the area would have been at that point in time had not the plant been in the area. Since, at any given point in time, a particular plant either is or is not in a particular area, it is not possible for any point in time to measure directly both employment in the presence of and in the absence of the plant. Hence, one of the two measurements must be made indirectly.

The choice of which of the two measurements must be made indirectly depends on whether the plant is or is not in the area at the time-point in which the researcher is interested. For example, it may be desired to obtain information regarding the employment effect which Plant A would have in a particular area if it were in that area at a specific time. The actual level of employment in the absence of Plant A would be directly measurable, while the level of employment in the area if Plant A were there at that time would have to be indirectly measured.

In the present study, the level of employment in the presence of the new plants in both areas was directly measurable. However, the level of employment which would have existed in the summer of 1966 in those areas in the absence of the plants was not directly measurable.

Indirect measurement of the direct employment effect of the new plants in both areas was carried out as follows. Each of the plant employees interviewed was asked to estimate how much per week he would have been able to earn in the study area at the time of interview, had not the plant been located in the area. He was then asked to indicate whether or not he would have remained at or come to work in the area for the alternative earnings which he had indicated he would have been able to obtain in the area at the time of interview if the plant had not been in the area. The direct employment effect of the new plant on that area was then computed as the number of plant employees who would have gone to work outside the area rather than work in the area for the alternative earnings which they had indicated they would have been able to obtain in the absence of the plant.

Each employee who had indicated that he would not have remained at (or come to) work in the two areas in the absence of the new plants was asked to indicate the place to which he would have gone. This information was used to estimate the proportion of the plant employees who would have left Ireland in the absence of the new plants in the study area.

2. Population

The magnitude of population migration into each area as a result of plant employees moving residence into the area in association with obtaining employment at the new plants was measured. It was assumed that, if the head of a household had moved into one of the areas in association with his obtaining of plant employment, the members of his household had migrated with him. It also was assumed that migration to the areas by plant employees who were non-heads of households involved only those plant employees.

In estimating the direct population effect of the new plants on the two areas, those employees who had indicated that they would have gone in search of employment to places outside the areas were classified on the basis of whether or not they were currently residing within the areas. Migration of heads of households currently residing within the areas who would have left the areas in the absence of the plants was assumed to involve the migration of the other members of their households, though possibly after some time lag. Migration of non-heads of households from the area was assumed to involve just themselves. The direct population effect on the two areas was estimated as the number of people who would have been involved in migration of households and of single people from the areas in the absence of the new plants.

3. Income

Each employee was asked to indicate whether or not there had been an increase in his household income as a result of his plant employment, after allowing for any expenses involved in his present job. Those employees who indicated that there had been such increases were asked to indicate the magnitude of the increments.

Each employee who had indicated that he would have gone to work outside the areas in the absence of the new plants was asked to indicate how much he felt he would have been earning in the alternative location had he gone there. A comparison of the present plant earnings of those employees who would have gone to work outside the areas in the absence of the plants with the earnings which they felt they would have been receiving in these alternative locations provided information of value in assessing the importance of any non-income considerations which prompted those employees to stay at work in the study areas rather than go to the alternative locations for the earnings which they believed they would have been able to receive in those alternative locations.

4. Expenditure

All plant employees who had reported an increase in household income as a result of plant employment were asked to allocate the actual or proposed expenditure of the reported increment in income among various expenditure categories. Some employees indicated the expenditure categories to which some of the increased income had been devoted. Others ranked expenditure categories by the amount of the added income devoted to them. Still others provided actual or percentage allocations of the added income among the expenditure categories.

Thus, it was possible to analyse the expenditure effects at three levels, viz. mentions of categories, rankings of categories and allocations among categories.

Plant employees reporting increased income were asked to indicate the town in which most of the income had been spent. Plant employees were also asked to indicate whether, as a result of obtaining plant employment, they or other members of their households had increased their shopping in the towns wherein the plants were situated. If so, they were asked to indicate whether or not they had decreased their shopping in other towns. The goods and services involved in such shopping shifts were then identified.

5. Farm business

The nature and magnitude of the direct effects on farm business in the two areas as a result of farm operators obtaining plant employment were identified by direct questioning of the farm operators involved. Each operator was asked whether or not there had been a change in a number of farm characteristics as a direct result of his obtaining plant employment. Each operator reporting a direct change in land utilization or in livestock numbers was asked to estimate the amount of the change which had occurred as a direct result of his obtaining plant employment.

E. SELECTIVITY FACTORS

In order to elucidate the nature and importance of any selectivity factors which influenced the obtaining of plant employment by certain people a number of comparisons were made between characteristics of groups of people in each area who obtained employment and corresponding groups of people who did not obtain employment at the new plants. Four groupings of people were considered for this purpose, farm operators, non-heads of farm households who were in the 14 to 64 year working age group, heads of urban households and, finally, non-heads of urban households who were in the working age group. Comparisons based on age and educational attainment were made in respect of each of these groups. Comparisons based on household size were also made for farm operators and for heads of urban households.

In addition, a large number of comparisons of farm business characteristics were made in respect of farm operators who had obtained employment at the new plants and other farm operators in the two areas who were not employed at the plants. In making these comparisons based on farm business characteristics, the direct effects of operator employment on these characteristics were taken into account in order to evaluate the selectivity factors in terms of original differences between the farm business characteristics of the two groups of farm operators, those who subsequently obtained plant employment and those who did not obtain such employment.

8

Employment Effects

This chapter presents an analysis of the direct employment effects of industrialization on the Tubbercurry and Scarriff areas. Specific attention is focused on new entrants to the labour force and their previous activities, the degree of transfer of labour to the new plants from agricultural occupations, the amount of entry of new employees to the areas in association with their plant employment and the numbers of plant employees who would have left the two areas in search of employment had they not obtained employment at the new plants. In addition, the prevalence of prior work in England among plant employees and the spatial incidence of employment effects are examined.

1. New entrants to the non-farm labour force

Table 23 shows the number of plant employees who entered the non-farm labour force for the first time in each area in taking

TABLE 23. Number of plant employees who entered non-farm labour force for first time in taking their present jobs

	Tubbercurry		Scarriff	
	Number	Per cent	Number	Per cent
Entered non-farm labour force for first time	91	58.0	48	31.8
Had been in non-farm labour force prior to present job	66	42.0	103	68.2
Total	157	100.0	151	100.0

their present jobs at the new industrial plants. In Tubbercurry, 91 plant employees or 58 per cent of the total number entered the non-farm labour force for the first time in taking jobs at the plant. This was a considerably higher proportion of plant employees than in Scarriff, where 48 employees or about 32 per cent of the plant employees entered the non-farm labour force for the first time to take their present jobs. It is therefore seen that in Tubbercurry only 42 per cent of plant employees had prior experience of non-farm jobs, as opposed to 68 per cent in Scarriff.

The immediately previous activity of the new entrants to the non-farm labour force is shown in table 24. The immediately

TABLE 24. Immediately previous activity of plant employees who entered the non farm labour force for the first time to accept plant employment

Immediately previous activity	Tubbercurry		Scarriff	
	Number	Per cent	Number	Per cent
Farm operator or agricultural contractor	16	17.6	8	16.7
Unpaid relative assisting on farm	3	3.3	14	29.1
Agricultural labourer	1	1.1	6	12.5
Total agricultural occupations	20	22.0	28	58.3
At school full-time	64	70.3	19	39.6
Engaged in home duties	5	5.5	—	—
Incapacitated	1	1.1	—	—
Not engaged in income-producing activity	1	1.1	1	2.1
Total non-agricultural activities	71	78.0	20	41.7
Subtotal	91	100.0	48	100.0
Previously in non-farm labour force	66	—	103	—
Total	157	—	151	—

previous activity of 16 of the new entrants in Tubbercurry was designated as farm operator or agricultural contractor. In contrast, only 8 of the new entrants in Scarriff were farm operators immediately prior to obtaining their present jobs. Thus, the other farm operators employed at the Scarriff plant did not enter the non-farm labour force for the first time to take jobs at the new plant. In Scarriff, considerably more people whose immediately previous activity was that of unpaid relative assisting on a farm entered the non-farm labour force for the first time than in Tubbercurry. Nearly 30 per cent of the new entrants in Scarriff belonged to this category, as opposed to 3.3 per cent in Tubbercurry. Similarly, 12.5 per cent of the new entrants in Scarriff had been hired agricultural labourers immediately previously, while only 1.1 per cent of the new entrants in Tubbercurry had been so engaged.

In all, 20 people or 22 per cent of the new entrants to the non-farm labour force in Tubbercurry and 28 people or 58 per cent of the new entrants in Scarriff had been engaged in agricultural occupations prior to their entry into the non-farm labour force. This, then, represents the degree to which people who were engaged wholly in agricultural occupations were attracted, either wholly or in part, into the non-farm labour force for the first time to work at the new plants.

Subtracting out these people, it is now seen that, in Tubbercurry, 71 people or 45.2 per cent of the employees entered the over-all labour force for the first time in taking their plant jobs, while 20 people or 13.2 per cent of the plant employees in Scarriff did so. Further reference to table 24 indicates the previous activity of these people. Practically all these new entrants to the labour force had been at school just prior to employment. The proportions involved were 90 per cent in Tubbercurry and 95 per cent in Scarriff. In Tubbercurry, 5 of the new entrants to the over-all labour force (7 per cent) had been engaged in home duties, while one person (1.5 per cent) had been unable to work because of health reasons and another person (1.5 per cent) had been unemployed immediately previously. Similarly, in Scarriff, one new entrant (2.1 per cent) to the total labour force had been unemployed immediately previously.

In summary, then, in both areas, there was a substantial number of new entrants to the non-farm labour force as a result of new employment opportunities at the new plants, the number being greater in Tubbercurry than in Scarriff. Some of these new entrants to the non-farm labour force had been gainfully employed in agricultural occupations, slightly over 20 per cent in Tubbercurry and nearly 60 per cent in Scarriff. Nearly all of the remaining new entrants had been at school full time prior to obtaining employment at the new plants.

2. Employee mobility into areas

Plant employees are classified in table 25 on the basis of their non-farm work association with the two areas of impact (AOI) defined in the study. In Tubbercurry, 25 of the 66 plant employees who had previously worked at non-farm jobs had always worked at such jobs in the AOI. In addition 5 plant employees had formerly worked outside the AOI and began to work in the AOI for the first time since 1956 at some jobs other than their present plants jobs. From these jobs, they later accepted employment at the new plant. There was also one plant employee who had worked in the AOI, then worked outside the AOI for some time, returning to work in the AOI at some stage since 1956, but not at his present plant job. These three groups of workers, 31 in all or 47 per cent of those who had previous non-farm jobs, had been working at other non-farm jobs in the Tubbercurry AOI immediately prior to obtaining jobs at the new plant.

In Scarriff, 57 plant employees or 45.3 per cent of the 103 who had previous non-farm work experience had been working at non-farm jobs within the AOI immediately prior to obtaining jobs at the new plant. This group comprised 49 people whose previous non-farm jobs had always been in the AOI, 6 whose jobs had always been outside the AOI until they began to work in the AOI subsequent to 1956 at a non-farm job other than at the new plant and 2 people who had worked originally in the AOI, then worked outside the AOI, but returned sometime after 1956 to work at some other non-farm job.

Employment at the new plants of these 31 Tubbercurry employees and 57 Scarriff employees who had been working immediately previously at other non-farm jobs within the two

TABLE 25. Distribution of plant employees by non-farm work association with area of impact (AOI)

Non-farm work association	Tubbercurry			Scarriff		
	Number	Per cent (n = 66)	Per cent (n = 157)	Number	Per cent (n = 103)	Per cent (n = 151)
Works in AOI at non-farm job now and has worked at prior non-farm job(s), always in AOI	25	37.9	15.9	49	47.6	32.5
Works in AOI at non-farm job now, worked outside AOI previously and began to work in AOI for first time since 1956, but not at present job	5	7.6	3.2	6	5.8	4.0
Works in AOI at non-farm job now, worked outside AOI previously and began to work in AOI since 1956, not at present job, but had worked in AOI at an earlier stage	1	1.5	0.6	2	1.9	1.3
Works in AOI at non-farm job now, worked outside AOI previously and began to work in AOI for first time at present job	25	37.9	15.9	29	28.2	19.2
Works in AOI at non-farm job now, worked outside AOI previously and began to work in AOI since 1956 at present job, but had worked in AOI at an earlier stage	10	15.1	6.4	17	16.5	11.2
Subtotal	66	100.0	42.0	103	100.0	68.2
Entered non-farm labour force for first time to take present job	91	—	58.0	48	—	31.8
Total	157	—	100.0	151	—	100.0

areas represents a shift of workers from other jobs within the two areas to employment at the new plants. If their former employers within the two areas hired other people to fill the jobs which these people vacated, such employment would be an indirect effect of industrialization. Information regarding the extent of replacement of workers who changed jobs in accepting employment at the new plants was not collected in the present study, which focused primarily on the direct effects. It may well be that some of these vacancies were not filled if the places of former employment were operating at less than full capacity. On the other hand, some additional people may have been drawn into the labour force for the first time to fill some of these posts, while further vacancies may have been filled by attracting some other people into the two areas. It is also possible that some of these jobs were filled by people who were working within the two areas at other jobs, which in turn would then be vacated. Hence, the indirect effect of industrialization on employment in both areas could spread throughout each area's employment pattern in a chain of employment adjustments.

However, 35 of the Tubbercurry employees or 53 per cent of those who had previous non-farm work experience had been working at jobs outside the AOI immediately prior to accepting their present plant employment. 25 of these employees began working in the AOI for the first time at their present jobs, while the other 10 had worked in the AOI at an earlier stage, had then gone to work outside the AOI, but had returned to work in the AOI at their present plant jobs.

Similarly, 46 of the Scarriff employees or 44.7 per cent of those who had previous non-farm work experience had been employed outside the AOI just prior to obtaining jobs at the new plant. 29 of these began working in the AOI for the first time at their plant jobs, while the other 17 had worked in the AOI at some stage previously, but had subsequently gone to work outside the AOI and recommenced working in the AOI at the new industrial plant.

These two latter groups, amounting to 22.3 per cent of all the

Tubbercurry employees interviewed and 30.4 per cent of the Scarriff employees interviewed, represent those people who were working outside the AOIs but were attracted into employment within the two AOIs following establishment of the new industrial plants. Some had worked earlier in the AOIs, but had left. Others hailed originally from the AOIs, but had left in search of their initial employment elsewhere, never having been employed earlier in the AOIs. Yet others had no previous association with the AOIs until acceptance of their present plant employment.

Finally, 4 of the 91 new entrants to the non-farm labour force in the Tubbercurry area came from outside the area, while 2 of the 46 new entrants in Scarriff came from outside the area to work at the new plant. These two groups of employees had had no previous association with the study areas.

3. Employment level in absence of plants

While the analysis conducted in the preceding subsections, in terms of the new entrants to the labour force and the employees attracted into the areas from outside sources of employment, provides information regarding the direct employment effects of the new industrial plants, the true magnitude of these direct effects is that obtained from a comparison of the existential levels of employment in the two areas with what the levels of employment would have been in those areas in the absence of the new plants.

This is a task fraught with many difficulties of measurement. One possibility would involve an estimation of what current employment in the absence of the new plants would be by reference to employment changes occurring during the period of interest in other initially similar areas which had not experienced industrialization. However, such a procedure was not possible in the present study.

The procedure adopted involved asking each employee for his estimate of how much he felt he could earn currently in the local areas if the new plant were not situated there. He was then asked whether or not he would have either remained in the area or come into the area to work for that wage. This procedure suffers from the limitation that no effective means exist whereby to assess the precision of the employees' estimates of their local income generating ability in the absence of the new plants. This limitation notwithstanding, it is believed that the procedure yields data which are of use in estimating the direct effects of industrialization.

As shown in table 26, 114 or 72.6 per cent of the employees in Tubbercurry said that they would not have remained in (or

TABLE 26. Distribution of plant employees by whether or not they would have remained to work in or entered to work in the area of impact for estimated alternative local wages

	Tubbercurry		Scarriff	
	Number	Per cent	Number	Per cent
Would have remained (or entered)	43	27.9	46	30.9
Would not have remained (or entered)	114	72.6	103	69.1
Subtotal	157	100.0	149	100.0
No information	—	—	2	—
Total	157	—	151	—

entered) the AOI to work for the alternative local wage which they felt they could earn in the AOI in the absence of the plant. Similarly, 103 people or 69.1 per cent of those who answered in Scarriff said that they would not now be working in that AOI if the new plant were not there.

This proportion, about 70 per cent, which was quite similar in both areas, provides an estimate of the direct effect of industrialization on employment in these two areas. Applying the observed proportions to the total number of plant employees in the two areas, the direct effects on employment may be estimated as an increase of 133 in employment in the Tubbercurry area and an increase of 134 in the Scarriff area. It is accordingly concluded that the hypothesis regarding a direct increase in employment in the two areas as a result of industrialization has been supported.

4. Prior employment in England

In Western Ireland, there has developed over a period of many years a strong pattern of emigration from local areas to England in search of employment. This emigration pattern has been a source of much concern, both at the local and national levels. It was felt by many people that the establishment of industrial plants in Western Ireland with the aid of grants paid under the Undeveloped Areas Act might, through employment effects, (a) reduce the number of people leaving Western Ireland to work in England and (b) induce a return to the West of Ireland of some former residents who had gone to England in search of employment and who might wish, for family or other reasons, to return to Western Ireland, provided some acceptable employment were available to them.

In order to shed some light on the extent to which the latter

TABLE 27. Distribution of plant employees by whether or not they had worked in England prior to obtaining plant employment

	Tubbercurry		Scarriff	
	Number	Per cent (n = 66)	Number	Per cent (n = 103)
Worked in England immediately prior to obtaining present job	18	27.3	13	12.6
Worked in England at an earlier stage, but not immediately prior to present job	9	13.6	9	8.7
Subtotal (worked in England at some stage prior to present job)	27	40.9	22	21.3
Never worked in England	39	59.1	81	78.7
Subtotal	66	100.0	103	100.0
Entered non-farm labour force for first time for present job	91	—	48	—
Total	157	—	151	—

aim may have been achieved, plant employees are classed in table 27 on the basis of whether or not they had worked in England prior to obtaining employment at the new industrial plants. In Tubbercurry, 27 people or 40.9 per cent of the employees who had previous non-farm work experience had worked in England at some stage previously. Eighteen of these had been working in England immediately prior to obtaining their present jobs; the other 9 had worked in England at some earlier stage. In Scarriff, 22 people or 21.3 per cent of the 103 employees who had previous non-farm work experience had worked in England, 13 of them immediately prior to obtaining employment at the new plant.

Those plant employees with previous work experience in England are classified in table 28 according to whether they had worked in the AOI at any stage. 15 of the 27 Tubbercurry employees

TABLE 28. Distribution of plant employees who had worked in England by previous work experience in the areas of impact prior to their present jobs

	Tubbercurry		Scarriff	
	Number	Per cent	Number	Per cent
Worked for first time in AOI at present job	15	55.6	6	27.3
Began working in AOI at present job, but had worked in AOI at an earlier stage (not immediately prior to present job)	6	22.2	11	50.0
Was working in AOI immediately prior to present job	6	22.2	5	22.7
Subtotal	27	100.0	22	100.0
Never worked in England	39	—	81	—
Not in non-farm labour force previously	91	—	48	—
Total	157	—	151	—

TABLE 29. Distribution by DED of Tubbercurry plant employees, new entrants to the non-farm labour force and plant employees who would not have remained to work in the area in the absence of the new plant

DED	Total employees	New entrants	Employees who would have left the area
Kilshalvey	5	2	3
Ballymote	3	1	3
Carrickbanagher	4	3	4
Achonry E.	6	5	3
Achonry W.	6	3	6
Aclare	1	1	1
Banada	16	13	6
Breencoragh	1	1	—
Branchfield	1	—	1
Coolaney	3	2	3
Temple	4	4	4
Owenmore	1	—	1
Cloonacool	6	3	5
Cloonoghill	3	1	2
Glendarragh	4	3	2
Kilturra	2	1	1
Leitrim	10	10	9
Streamstown	3	3	1
Tubbercurry	65	28	50
Cloonmore	2	—	2
Doocastle	3	2	2
Kilbeagh	2	1	1
Sonnagh	2	1	2
Subtotal	153	88	110
Reside outside area	4	3	4
Total	157	91	114

who had worked in England began working for the first time in the AOI at their present jobs, 6 or 22 per cent were working at other jobs in the AOI just prior to obtaining their plant jobs, while 6 employees who had worked in England had worked in the AOI at an earlier stage in their careers and had come back to work in the AOI at the present jobs. It is therefore seen that the new plant directly attracted back 18 employees who had been working in England, to work in the Tubbercurry area.

Similarly, 13 employees were directly attracted back to work in the Scarriff area by the new plant, 11 of whom had worked in the AOI at some earlier stage. Five of the Scarriff employees who had worked in England were working at other occupations in the AOI immediately prior to obtaining employment at the new plant.

This evidence indicates that the new plants did attract back some employees who had left those areas in search of employment in England, but that the major employment effects of the new plants operated through increasing employment in the two areas by providing employment opportunities for people who would probably have otherwise left the two areas rather than by attracting back former residents of the areas to work in the new plants.

5. Spatial distribution of plant employment

Plant employees in Tubbercurry are classified in table 29 according to the DED of their residence. 4 of the 157 employees reside outside the AOI. 65 or 42.5 per cent of the 153 plant employees who reside within the AOI are residents of the Tubbercurry DED. The DEDs of Banada and Leitrim, both of which adjoin the Tubbercurry DED, contain 16 and 10 plant employees respectively. Thus, residents of these three DEDs comprise 91 or nearly 60 per cent of the employees who resided within the AOI.

The distribution of the residences of plant employees among DEDs in both areas is depicted in figure 6, while the DED distribution of the Scarriff employees is shown in table 30. As will be noted, 58 or 42.3 per cent of the 137 employees residing within the Scarriff AOI were residents of the Scarriff DED, the next highest number being 14 from the adjoining DED of Ogonnelloe. Relatively high numbers of employees resided in the DEDs of Drumaan, Kilseily and Killaloe. These DEDs contain the towns of Whitegate, Broadford and Killaloe respectively.

These data indicate that plant employment in the Tubbercurry area was more concentrated in and around the town where the plant was situated than was the case in the Scarriff area. Further evidence to support this viewpoint is presented in table 31 which

TABLE 30. Distribution by DED of Scarriff plant employees, new entrants to the non-farm labour force and plant employees who would not have remained to work in the area in the absence of the new plant

DED	Total employees	New entrants	Employees who would have left the area
Kieseily	11	1	8
Carrowbaun	1	—	1
Killaloe	9	1	8
Ogonnelloe	14	8	2
Ayle	2	2	1
Boherglass	5	3	2
Cahermurphy	1	—	1
Cloonusker	3	2	1
Corlea	1	—	1
Feakle	7	1	3
Cappaghbaun	4	3	2
Drummaan	13	2	11
Iniscaltra N.	2	—	2
Mountshannon	3	2	2
Scarriff	58	19	38
Glandree	1	—	—
Killaneena	1	—	1
Loughea	1	1	—
Subtotal	137	45	92
Reside outside area	14	3	11
Total	151	48	103

TABLE 31. Distribution of plant employees by distance of residence from plant

Distance (miles)	Tubbercurry		Scarriff	
	Number	Per cent	Number	Per cent
Under 4	91	58.3	67	44.7
4 and under 8	38	24.4	29	19.3
8 and under 12	14	9.0	44	29.4
12 and under 16	8	5.1	6	4.0
16 and under 20	2	1.3	2	1.3
Subtotal	156	100.0	150	100.0
No information	1	—	1	—
Total	157	—	151	—
Mean distance from plant	4.31 miles		5.20 miles	

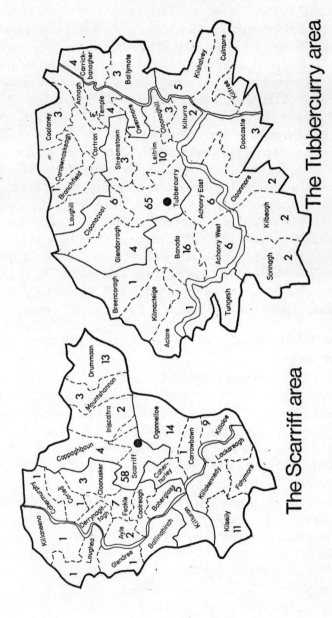

Figure 6.   Distribution of the residences of plant employees among District Electoral Divisions

shows the distribution of plant employees by distance from the new plants. In the Tubbercurry AOI, nearly 60 per cent of the employees resided within 4 miles of the new plant, as compared to about 45 per cent of the Scarriff employees. Similarly more of the Tubbercurry employees than of the Scarriff employees resided between 4 and 8 miles from the plant. However, nearly 30 per cent of the Scarriff employees resided between 8 and 12 miles from the plant, as compared to 9 per cent of the Tubbercurry employees. The three other towns in the Scarriff AOI mentioned earlier all fall in this range. Many of the plant employees who resided in these towns were former residents of these towns who had returned to these towns when employment became available at the new plant. For example, about half of the plant employees who resided in Killaloe and in Whitegate had returned from outside the area and had recommenced residence in their old home towns. In both areas, well over 90 per cent of the employees resided within 12 miles of the new plants. The mean distance of residence from the plant was 4.31 miles for the Tubbercurry employees and 5.20 miles for the Scarriff employees.

6. Spatial distribution of new entrants to non-farm labour force

The distribution among DEDs of the new entrants to the non-farm labour force in the two areas is shown in tables 29 and 30. Similarly, this distribution is depicted in figure 7. In the Tubbercurry AOI, the DEDs of Tubbercurry, Ogonnelloe and Leitrim contain 51 or 58 per cent of the 88 new entrants to the non-farm labour force who were residents of the AOI, while no other DED contained more than 5 such new entrants. The proportion of the new entrants who were residents of those 3 DEDs (58 per cent) is practically the same as the proportion of plant employees who resided in the same DEDs (60 per cent), indicating that the new entrants were spatially distributed relative to the new plant in approximately the same manner as were the other plant employees.

In the Scarriff AOI, 19 of the 45 new entrants to the non-farm

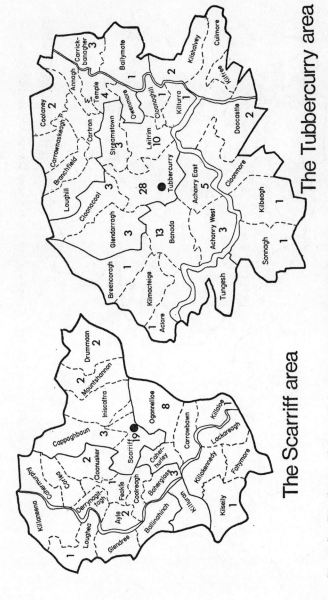

Figure 7. Distribution of the residences of new entrants to the non-farm labour force among District Electoral Divisions

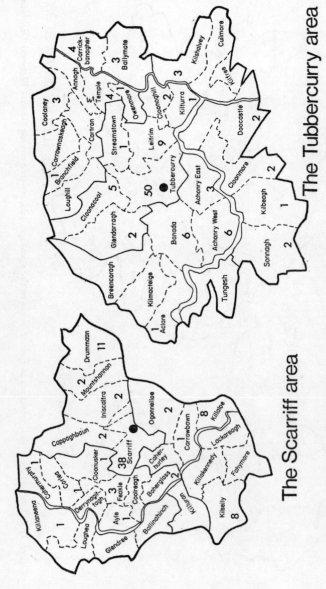

Figure 8. Distribution of direct employment effect of the new plants among District Electoral Divisions

labour force who were residents of the AOI were residents of the Scarriff DED. This number amounted to 42.2 per cent of the new entrants, and may be compared with the fact noted earlier that 42.3 per cent of the Scarriff employees resided in the Scarriff DED. Hence, it may be concluded that the geographical distribution of new entrants to the non-farm labour force was similar to the distribution of all plant employees in both areas, the incidence being greatest in the DEDs in which the new plants were situated.

7. Spatial distribution of employees who would have left to work elsewhere

Tables 29 and 30 and figure 8 show the distribution by DED of those employees who would not have remained to work in the AOIs in the absence of the new plants. In the case of the Tubbercurry plant, 4 of the 114 such employees resided outside of the AOI. 50 or 45.5 per cent of the 110 who resided within the AOI were residents of the Tubbercurry DED. This is slightly higher than the 42.5 per cent of employees who resided in the Tubbercurry DED. The DEDs of Tubbercurry, Banada and Leitrim accounted for 65 or 59.1 per cent of the employees who would have left to seek work elsewhere, compared with the 60 per cent of plant employees who resided within these DEDs.

These employees who would have gone to work elsewhere are classified in table 32 by distance of residence from the new plants. Nearly 60 per cent of the Tubbercurry group resided within 4

TABLE 32. Distribution of plant employees who would have left both areas in the absence of the new plants by distance of present residence from plant

Distance from plant (miles)	Tubbercurry		Scarriff	
	Number	Per cent	Number	Per cent
Under 6	66	57.9	46	44.7
4 and under 8	26	22.8	15	14.5
8 and under 12	10	8.8	35	34.0
12 and under 16	7	6.1	4	3.9
16 and under 20	2	1.8	1	1.0
20 and over	3	2.6	2	1.9
Total	114	100.0	103	100.0

miles of the plant, while about 45 per cent of the Scarriff
employees did so. In the Tubbercurry area the employment effect
declined steadily as distance from Tubbercurry increased. However, in Scarriff, 35 people or one third of those who would have
left the AOI to seek work elsewhere in the absence of the plant
resided between 8 and 12 miles from the Scarriff plant. This
number includes those former residents of Killaloe and Whitegate
who had returned to those towns following the opening up of
new employment opportunities in the area. It also includes other
residents of those towns who indicated that they would have left
the area in the absence of the new plant because of the absence
of suitable alternative employment opportunities in those towns.
In a sense, therefore, those towns have been serving as dormitory
towns for many of the Scarriff plant employees.

8. Alternative employment locations

All plant employees who had indicated that, in the absence of
the new plants, they would have left the study areas in search of
employment were asked to indicate where they would have gone
in search of such employment. As shown in table 33, over two
thirds of the Tubbercurry employees who would not have
remained to work in the AOI would have sought employment in
England. This is a substantially higher proportion than the 45
per cent of those from the Scarriff area who would have sought
employment in England. Both areas are approximately the same
distance from England. Yet, historically, there has been a substantially more pronounced pattern of emigration to England
from the northwestern counties, such as Sligo, in which the
Tubbercurry plant is situated, than from areas like East Clare,
in which Scarriff is situated.

Exactly why these differential emigration patterns have developed historically is not clear. Part of the explanation may lie in
the fact that the city of Limerick, containing over 50,000 people,
is about 25 miles distance from Scarriff, in an adjoining county.
No such city occurs in any of the counties adjoining Co. Sligo.
As a result of this, it is seen that 15 per cent of the Scarriff group

TABLE 33. Places to which employees who would have left the two areas would have gone

Place	Tubbercurry		Scarriff	
	Number	Per cent	Number	Per cent
Same county (excluding Shannon)	5	4.4	3	3.1
Adjoining county	4	3.5	15	15.3
Other western county	2	1.8	—	—
Dublin	10	8.8	20	20.4
Rest of Ireland	3	2.6	—	—
Great Britain	77	67.5	44	44.9
United States of America	8	7.0	6	6.1
Shannon	—	—	9	9.2
Other (including further study or religious life)	5	4.4	1	1.0
Subtotal	114	100.0	98	100.0
No information regarding where employee would have gone	—	—	5	—
No information regarding whether or not employee would have left the area	—	—	2	—
Would not have left the area	43	—	46	—
Total	157	—	151	—

would have sought employment in an adjoining county, while only 3.5 per cent of the Tubbercurry group would have done so. However, there are also other factors of importance in explaining the differential emigration pattern, since 20 per cent of the Scarriff employees who would have left would have gone to Dublin, while only 8.8 per cent of the Tubbercurry group would have done so, even though both areas are about 120 miles from Dublin. About 10 per cent of the Scarriff employees would have gone to work at the Shannon Airport Industrial Estate. The proportion who would have gone to the United States for employment was approximately the same in both areas.

In summary, about three quarters of the Tubbercurry employees who would not have been at work in the AOI in the absence of the new plant would have sought employment outside Ireland, while about half of the corresponding Scarriff group would also have left Ireland in search of employment.

9

Population Effects

In this chapter the residence association of plant employees with the two areas of impact is examined in section A. The magnitude of migration into the areas following industrialization is measured in section B and finally, in section C, the population effects of the new industrial plants on the two areas are estimated in terms of the levels of population which would currently exist in both areas in the absence of the new plants.

A. RESIDENCE ASSOCIATION WITH AREAS OF IMPACT

Plant employees are classified in table 34 according to their residence association with the two areas. About three quarters of the Tubbercurry employees and two thirds of the Scarriff employees have resided within the two areas continuously since 1956. 7 employees moved into the Tubbercurry AOI since 1956, but these moves were not associated with the taking of their present jobs. Similarly, 5 plant employees moved into the Scarriff AOI since 1956, but not in association with obtaining employment at the new plant. Thus, 123 people or 78 per cent of the Tubbercurry employees were local residents at the time they obtained plant employment and 107 or 71 per cent of the Scarriff employees were residents of that AOI when they obtained plant employment.

In Tubbercurry, 18 plant employees moved residence into the AOI for the first time in association with obtaining plant employment, while 12 other employees moved residence into the AOI

TABLE 34. Distribution of plant employees by residence association with the areas of impact

Residence Association	Tubbercurry		Scarriff	
	Number	Per cent	Number	Per cent
Lives in AOI and has done so since 1956	116	73.9	102	67.5
Lives in AOI but has moved into AOI for first time since 1956, not associated with present job	4	2.5	2	1.3
Lives in AOI, has moved into AOI since 1956, not associated with present job, but formerly resided in AOI	3	1.9	3	2.0
Lives in AOI, but moved into AOI for first time since 1956, associated with present job	18	11.5	11	7.3
Lives in AOI, has moved into AOI since 1956, associated with present job, but formerly resided in AOI	12	7.7	19	12.6
Lives outside AOI, but lived in AOI at some stage since 1956	—	—	2	8.0
Lives outside AOI and has done so since 1956	4	2.5	12	8.0
Total	157	100.0	151	100.0

in association with obtaining plant employment, but had resided in the AOI during some former period. 11 of the Scarriff employees moved residence into that AOI for the first time associated with obtaining jobs at the new plant, while 19 former residents of the AOI moved residence back to the AOI in association with obtaining employment at the new plant. Thus, in each AOI 30 plant employees moved residence into the AOI in association with their new plant employment.

Four Tubbercurry employees currently reside outside the AOI, while 14 Scarriff employees reside outside the AOI. As discussed earlier, 9 of the latter reside in Ballina, Co. Tipperary, which is connected to Killaloe by a bridge across the Shannon, while 4 more reside elsewhere in Tipperary, being also excluded, by definition, from the AOI.

B.   MIGRATION INTO AREAS OF IMPACT

As noted in the previous section, 30 employees moved residence into each AOI in association with their plant employment. The population impact of these residence changes is examined in this section. 20 of the 30 employees who moved residence into the Tubbercurry AOI were heads of households, while 25 of the 30 who moved into the Scarriff AOI were heads of households.

Since a migration of heads of households into both areas occurred, the increase in population which resulted was greater than the number of employees who migrated into the AOIs. As shown in table 35, the migration of heads of households into the Tubbercurry AOI resulted in an increase of 63 persons in the population of the area, that of the 10 non-heads resulting in an increase of a further 10, thus giving an increase of 73 persons as

TABLE 35. Distribution of people who migrated into areas of impact in association with heads of households obtaining plant employment by size of household together with number of migrating employees who were non-heads of households

Size of household (persons)	Tubbercurry		Scarriff	
	Households	People	Households	People
1	7	7	4	4
2	1	2	1	2
3	2	6	7	21
4	5	20	6	24
5	2	10	2	10
6	3	18	3	18
7	—	—	—	—
8	—	—	1	8
9	—	—	1	9
Subtotal	20	63	25	96
Non-heads of households	—	10	—	5
Total	—	73	—	101

a result of migration into the Tubbercurry AOI in association
with the obtaining of plant employment by these 30 employees.

Similarly in Scarriff, migration of 25 heads of households into
the AOI gave rise to an increase of 96 persons, while there were
5 non-heads of households who migrated to the AOI giving an
increase of 101 persons in the AOI as a result of migration of
these 30 plant employees to the AOI in association with obtaining
employment at the new plant.

The geographical incidence of this increase was also examined.
As hypothesized, a large proportion of these increases occurred
in and around Tubbercurry and Scarriff. In fact, 54 persons or
74 per cent of the 73 people involved in the migration into the
Tubbercurry AOI were residing in the Tubbercurry DED when
interviewed, while none of the other 32 DEDs in the Tubbercurry
AOI had received more than an increase of 6.

Of the increase of 101 people in the Scarriff AOI, 49 persons
were residing in the Scarriff DED, 24 in the Killaloe DED and
12 in the Drummaan DED. These 3 DEDs contain the towns of
Scarriff, Killaloe and Whitegate, respectively. The remaining 16
people were residents of 4 other DEDs (one household per DED).
It is thus seen that a greater proportion of the migration into the
AOI associated with plant employment was concentrated in and
close to the town where the plant was located in the Tubbercurry
AOI than in the Scarriff AOI, where some of the migrants to
the AOI settled in other towns within the area. Practically all
of the migration into the towns of Killaloe and Whitegate was
associated with the return to these towns of former residents who
had left these towns at an earlier stage but returned to their old
home towns when employment became available at the Scarriff
plant.

C.   POPULATION IN THE ABSENCE OF THE NEW PLANTS

As noted in the previous chapter, a large proportion of the
employees of both plants said that they would not have remained
to work in the AOI for the alternative earnings which they felt

they could have obtained locally, if the new plants had not been established.

These employees are classified in table 36 on the basis of whether or not they are heads of households or other household

TABLE 36. Distribution of plant employees who would not have remained in the areas of impact for the alternative local earnings expected in the absence of the new plants by status within their households

Household status	Tubbercurry		Scarriff	
	Number	Per cent	Number	Per cent
Head of household residing in AOI	37	33.6	46	50.0
Other household member residing in AOI	73	66.4	46	50.0
Subtotal	110	100.0	92	100.0
Reside outside AOI	4	—	11	—
Total	114	—	103	—

members residing within the two areas. 110 such employees currently reside within the Tubbercurry AOI and 92 within the Scarriff AOI. One third of the former and one half of the latter are heads of households. It was assumed that when a head of household would move residence from the AOI, the other members of his household would also move, though there might be some lags present in this connection.

Table 37 shows the direct population reduction which would occur if these households migrated from the two areas, along with the reduction involved as a result of the migration of plant employees who were non-heads of households. Migration of 37 household heads from the Tubbercurry area would have resulted in a population reduction of 125 persons, while that of plant employees who were non-heads of households would have reduced population by a further 73 persons, giving a total population reduction of 198 people.

TABLE 37. Distribution of households and people who would not be residents of the areas of impact if industrialization had not occurred classified by household size

Household size	Tubbercurry		Scarriff	
	Households	People	Households	People
1	7	7	7	7
2	8	16	3	6
3	5	15	8	24
4	7	28	8	32
5	5	25	8	40
6	3	18	5	30
7	1	7	3	21
8	—	—	—	—
9	1	9	2	18
10	—	—	2	20
Subtotal	37	125	46	198
Non-heads of households	—	73	—	46
Total	—	198	—	244

In the Scarriff AOI, a population loss of 198 persons would have resulted from migration of the 46 heads of households and a further loss of 46 from migration of plant employees who are non-heads of households. Thus the Scarriff area would have experienced a population loss of 244 people.

Assuming that the population effect of plant employment was similar in the case of the plant employees who were not interviewed, one may estimate the direct population effects of industrialization in the two areas as an increase of 231 in the population of the Tubbercurry AOI and an increase of 318 in the population of the Scarriff AOI. These increases have been measured relative to the level at which it was estimated that the population of these two areas would be in 1966 in the absence of the new industrial plants.

It must be borne in mind that these estimates represent the direct effect of plant employment on population levels in these two areas. The total population effect may be expected to be greater for a number of reasons. First of all, the study dealt only with employees up through the rank of working foreman. As most of the plant management personnel had come from outside the two areas, it may be expected that they and their families would not have been currently residing in the areas had not the plants been established. Secondly, indirect employment effects may be expected to have occurred. These may, in turn, be expected to have given rise to indirect population effects. For example, some proprietors of small businesses in the two areas might have been able to stay in business after the plants had been located in these areas, whereas otherwise they might have been forced out of business as a result of the lower population which would have otherwise been in the areas. These people might have then been obliged to leave the areas in search of employment.

The direct population effect of the new industrialization was estimated to be greater in the Scarriff area than in the Tubbercurry area during the period under study. This reflects the fact that relatively more heads of households obtained employment in the Scarriff plant than in Tubbercurry. It is thus estimated that instead of its actual level of 16,793, the 1966 population of the Tubbercurry AOI would have been not more than 16,562 in the absence of the industrialization. Similarly, it is estimated that in the absence of the Scarriff industrial plant, the 1966 population of the Scarriff AOI would have been not more than 7,254, instead of the actual 1966 population of 7,572.

D. SPATIAL INCIDENCE OF POPULATION EFFECTS

In order to examine the spatial incidence within the two areas of the direct population effects of industrialization, the direct population effect generated by the plant employment of those employees who were interviewed was distributed among DEDs in the two areas as shown in figure 9.

In the Tubbercurry area, the direct population effect of the plant employment of the interviewees amounted to 1.18 per cent of the 1966 population of the area. However, if one considers the DEDs in the Rural District of Tubbercurry, this effect amounted to 1.97 per cent of the population of the Rural District. Both in

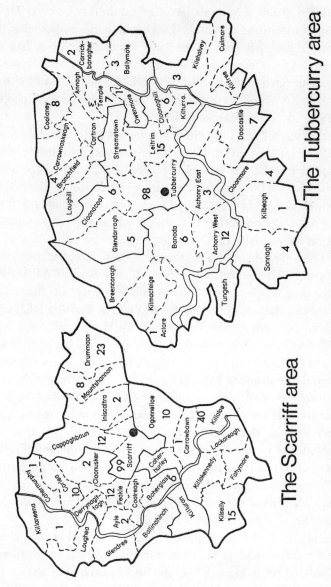

Figure 9. Distribution of direct population effect of the new plants among District Electoral Divisions

terms of absolute numbers and as a proportion of the 1966 population, the direct population effect on the Tubbercurry DED was higher than on any other DED within the area, being 98 persons or 5.41 per cent of the 1966 population. Thus, half of the population effect of the Tubbercurry industrial development was concentrated in the Tubbercurry DED. The DEDs of Leitrim and Achonry West had the next highest numbers of people involved, 15 and 12 respectively.

In the Scarriff area, the direct population effect resulting from the plant employment of those employees who were interviewed amounted to 3.22 per cent of the 1966 population of the area. Within the DEDs contained in the Scarriff Rural District, it amounted to 4.11 per cent. Once again, both in absolute numbers and as a proportion of the 1966 population, the direct population effect on the Scarriff DED was higher than on any other DED within the area, being 99 persons or 8.92 per cent of the 1966 population. The population effect on the Scarriff DED was slightly over 40 per cent of the population effect on the whole area. About one sixth of the effect was on the Killaloe DED and about 10 per cent on the Drummaan DED.

This evidence, particularly that in the Tubbercurry area, supports the hypotheses that the population effect of industrialization would be strongest in and close to the towns wherein the new plants were situated. However, in the Scarriff area, concentrations of the population effect in DEDs containing other towns were greater than in the Tubbercurry area.

It is also of interest to examine the direct population effect of plant employment on the towns within the two areas. In the Tubbercurry area, the population effect on towns was 92 persons or 46.5 per cent of the total, while in the Scarriff area it was 125 persons or 51.2 per cent of the total.

Table 38 shows the population effect on each town of the employment of those persons who were interviewed at the plants. The bulk of the urban population effect in each area was on the two towns wherein the new plants were situated. It is estimated that in the absence of the new plants the population of Tubber-

TABLE 38. Distribution of direct population effect of industrialization among towns

	Actual 1966 population	Population effect of industry	
		Estimated number	Per cent of 1966 population
Tubbercurry Area			
Ballymote	921	3	0.33
Charlestown-Bellaghy	680	5	0.73
Coolaney	117	7	5.98
Tubbercurry	937	77	8.22
Scarriff Area			
Broadford	158	5	3.16
Killaloe	816	21	2.57
Feakle	121	4	3.31
Whitegate	169	8	4.73
Mountshannon	149	8	5.37
Scarriff	673	79	11.74

curry would have been at least 8.22 per cent less than its 1966 level of 937, while that of Scarriff would have been at least 11.74 per cent less than its 1966 population of 673 persons. The population effects reported in table 38 refer only to those employees who were interviewed. Hence, the full magnitude of the direct effect attributable to all employees would be greater. Furthermore, the direct population effect due to the management personnel of the new plants would have been concentrated in Scarriff and Tubbercurry. In addition, it is reasonable to expect that important indirect population effects had also occurred to a greater extent in the towns of Scarriff and Tubbercurry than elsewhere in the two areas.

Income Effects

The direct income effects of plant employment are examined in this chapter, which contains four sections. Section A contains a descriptive analysis of the present earnings of plant employees. The alternative local earnings expected by plant employees in the absence of the new plants are discussed in section B, while section C contains an analysis of the alternative earnings expected elsewhere by plant employees who would have sought work outside the two areas had not the new plants been located in those areas. A comparison between these earnings expected elsewhere and the present plant earnings of the employees who would have left the two areas provides information regarding the importance of any non-income considerations prompting these employees to remain in the two areas. Finally, in section D the amount and spatial incidence of net increments to household income arising directly from industrial employment are examined.

A.   PRESENT EARNINGS OF PLANT EMPLOYEES

The distribution of plant employees by their present weekly plant earnings is shown in table 39. Certain differences are immediately apparent. The distribution of weekly earnings of the Tubbercurry plant employees exhibits a considerably larger variability than does the distribution of weekly earnings of the Scarriff employees. Nearly two thirds of the Scarriff employees receive wages in the £8 to £12 category, while the greatest proportion of Tubbercurry

TABLE 39. Distribution of plant employees by weekly plant earnings

Weekly earnings (£)	Tubbercurry		Scarriff	
	Number	Per cent	Number	Per cent
Under 4	25	15.9	1	0.7
4 and under 8	54	34.6	11	7.3
8 and under 12	29	18.5	95	63.4
12 and under 16	16	10.2	20	13.3
16 and under 20	9	5.7	16	10.7
20 and under 24	17	10.8	5	3.3
24 and under 28	4	2.5	2	1.3
28 and under 32	3	1.9	—	—
Subtotal	157	100.0	150	100.0
No information	—	—	2	—
Total	157	—	151	—
Mean weekly earnings (£)	10.0		11.3	
Median weekly earnings (£)	7.9		10.5	
Modal weekly earnings (£)	5 and under 6		10 and under 11	

employees in any wage category is slightly over one third in the £4 to £8 category.

This greater variability of wages among the Tubbercurry employees is largely explained by the lower occupational homogeneity of the Tubbercurry employees and by sex differentials in wages. For example, about 16 per cent of the Tubbercurry employees had weekly earnings of less than £4, as compared with less than 1 per cent of the employees in Scarriff. This reflects the larger number of apprentices hired in Tubbercurry. Similarly, over 15 per cent of the Tubbercurry employees received weekly wages of over £20, compared with 4.6 per cent of the Scarriff employees, reflecting the larger number of skilled plant employees who were working in Tubbercurry. The presence of 35 per cent of the Tubbercurry employees in the £4 to £8 category, as opposed to 7 per cent in Scarriff, is largely explained by the larger number of female plant employees in Tubbercurry.

The mean weekly wage of plant employees interviewed was £11.3 in Scarriff and £10.0 in Tubbercurry. The median weekly wage was £10.5 in Scarriff and £7.9 in Tubbercurry. The modal weekly wage was between £10 and £11 in Scarriff and between £5 and £6 in Tubbercurry. Thus, mean, median and modal weekly wages were higher in the case of the Scarriff employees than those of the Tubbercurry employees.

Mean weekly earnings of the Tubberburry employees classified by farm work association and by sex are shown in table 40. For

TABLE 40. Mean weekly plant earnings (£) of Tubbercurry plant employees classified by farm work association and by sex

Farm work association[a]	Sex		Total
	Male	Female	
FO–FO	11.9 (n = 15)	—	11.9 (n = 15)
FW–FW	7.4 (n = 30)	5.2 (n = 16)	6.6 (n = 46)
FW–NFWA	12.3 (n = 14)	5.4 (n = 4)	10.7 (n = 18)
NFWA–NFWA	13.2 (n = 53)	5.9 (n = 20)	11.2 (n = 73)
Total	11.6 (n = 116)	5.6 (n = 41)	10.0 (n = 157)

[a] An explanation of the farm work association symbols appears on this page.

convenience in the tabular presentation, this table and all subsequent tables in which the farm work association of plant employees in either area is depicted, symbols are used to denote the various farm work association categories. The symbol FO stands for "farm operator"; FW stands for "non-operator farm worker"; NFWA stands for "no farm work association". Plant employees are classified on the basis of their farm work association at the time of obtaining plant employment and at the present time. Various combinations of the three symbols will be used to denote the nine possible combinations of farm work association. Thus, for example, FO-FO means "farm operator at the time of obtaining plant employment and is farm operator now", FW-NFWA means "non-operator farm worker at the time of obtaining plant employment and has no farm work association now". Other combinations are formed in like manner. Because of the possibility of disclosure of financial data pertaining to individual plant employees, such data are not presented separately in table 40 or in subsequent similar tables for farm work association groups which contain only one or a few employees. However, data pertaining to such employees are included in the totals shown for the two areas.

In all categories of farm work association, plant wages of female employees in Tubbercurry were substantially lower than those of male employees. The mean weekly wage of male employees was £11.6 while that of female employees was £5.6, less than half of that received by male employees. There was extremely little variability in the wages of female employees according to farm work association.

The mean weekly wage of the 15 male farm operators who did not change their farm work association was £11.9, as compared with a mean weekly wage of £13.2 for the 53 male employees who had no farm work association at any stage. Mean wages of farm operators were higher than those of male non-operator farm workers who did not change their farm work status following plant employment, while mean wages of non-operator farm workers who severed their farm work association were slightly higher than those of the farm operators. However, all these groups had mean weekly wages which were lower than those of the group who had no farm work association.

TABLE 41. Mean weekly plant earnings (£) of Scarriff plant employees classified by farm work association and by sex

Farm work association[a]	Sex		Total
	Male	Female	
FO–FO	10.9 (n = 17)	—	10.9 (n = 17)
FW–FW	9.7 (n = 28)	7.3 (n = 3)	9.5 (n = 31)
FW–NFWA	10.7 (n = 11)	b	10.4 (n = 12)
NFWA–NFWA	12.4 (n = 81)	7.6 (n = 5)	12.1 (n = 86)
Total	11.5 (n = 141)	7.5 (n = 9)	11.3 (n = 150)

[a] An explanation of the farm work association symbols appears on p. 136.
[b] This cell contains only one employee.

Similar data in respect of the Scarriff employees are presented in table 41. The mean weekly wage of the 17 male farm operators who did not change their farm work association following acceptance of their plant employment was £10.9. As in Tubbercurry, wages of non-operator farm workers who retained their farm work status were lower than those of the farm operators, but wages of non-operator farm workers who severed their farm work association were about the same as those of the farm operators. However, the wages of all three groups were below those of the employees who had no farm work association.

As in the case of the Tubbercurry employees, mean weekly wages of female plant employees (£7.5) were below those of male plant employees (£11.5). Once again, there was hardly any variation in mean wages of female plant employees according to farm work association.

In comparing the mean weekly wages of plant employees in the two areas, it is seen that the mean wage of farm operators in Tubbercurry (£11.9) was £1 higher than that of the farm operators in the Scarriff plant. Similarly, mean wages of male employees in Tubbercurry who had no farm work association (£13.2) were about £1 higher than the wages of the Scarriff employees who had no farm work association (£12.4). Thus, the differential between the wages of farm operators employed at the plants and the wages of male plant employees who had no farm work association was approximately the same in both areas.

Mean wages paid to female employees in Tubbercurry were substantially below the mean wages paid to female employees in the Scarriff plant. This difference is mainly due to the fact that female employees in Scarriff were almost all engaged in clerical or secretarial positions, while most of those in Tubbercurry were production workers. Wages paid to female employees in clerical and secretarial positions are usually larger in Ireland than wages paid to female plant production workers. Wages paid to female clerical and secretarial workers in Tubbercurry were similar to those paid to the female clerical and secretarial employees in Scarriff.

B. ALTERNATIVE LOCAL EARNINGS

Each of the plant employees was asked to estimate the alternative weekly earnings which he could currently obtain locally if the new plant were not in the area. Plant employees are distributed in table 42 according to their estimates of alternative local weekly

TABLE 42. Distribution of plant employees by estimated alternative local weekly earnings in the absence of the plant

Estimated alternative local weekly earnings (£)	Tubbercurry		Scarriff	
	Number	Per cent	Number	Per cent
Zero	76	48.4	71	47.7
Under 4	28	17.8	7	4.7
4 and under 8	37	23.6	33	22.1
8 and under 12	11	7.0	31	20.8
12 and over	5	3.2	7	4.7
Subtotal	157	100.0	149	100.0
No information	—	—	2	—
Total	157	—	151	—
Mean alternative earnings (£)	2.90		4.00	
Median alternative earnings (£)	2.20		3.25	
Modal alternative earnings (£)	0.00		0.00	

earnings in the absence of the new plants. In both areas, practically the same proportion of employees (48.4 per cent in Tubbercurry and 47.7 per cent in Scarriff) felt that in the absence of the plants they would not be able to earn anything locally.

Among those who felt they could obtain positive earnings locally, the Tubbercurry employees tended to give lower estimates of the alternative earnings which they could obtain than did the Scarriff employees. The mean alternative local earnings estimated by the Scarriff employees was £4.0, while that of the Tubbercurry employees was £2.9, about £1 less. Similarly, the median alternative local earnings expected by the Scarriff employees was £3.25, while that expected by the Tubbercurry employees was £2.20.

Mean alternative local earnings are shown in table 43 for the

Tubbercurry plant employees, classified by farm association and by sex. The 15 farm operators who did not change their farm work association expected mean alternative local weekly earnings of £3.8, about £1 more than that expected by the 53 male plant

TABLE 43. Mean alternative local weekly earnings (£) expected in the absence of the new plant by Tubbercurry plant employees classified by farm work association and by sex

Farm work association[a]	Sex		Total
	Male	Female	
FO–FO	3.8 (n = 15)	—	3.8 (n = 15)
FW–FW	2.6 (n = 30)	3.0 (n = 16)	2.7 (n = 46)
FW–NFWA	3.6 (n = 14)	3.9 (n = 4)	3.7 (n = 18)
NFWA–NFWA	2.9 (n = 53)	1.8 (n = 20)	2.6 (n = 73)
Total	3.0 (n = 116)	2.5 (n = 41)	2.9 (n = 117)

[a] An explanation of the farm work association symbols appears on p. 136.

employees who had no farm work association at any stage. Alternative earnings expected by the farm operators were higher than those expected by male plant employees who were non-operator farm workers at the time they obtained plant employment.

The mean alternative weekly earnings expected by male plant employees (£3.0) was higher than that expected by female plant employees (£2.5), though the female plant employees exhibited more variability according to farm association in their expectations than appeared in their present earnings.

Corresponding data pertaining to the Scarriff employees are presented in table 44. Farm operators expected higher mean alternative weekly earnings (£5.6) than did the male employees who had no farm work association (£3.9). As in the case of Tubbercurry, the mean alternative local weekly earnings expected by farm operators were higher than were expected by plant employees who were non-operator farm workers when they obtained plant employment.

TABLE 44. Mean alternative local weekly earnings (£) expected in the absence of the new plant by Scarriff plant employees classified by farm work association and by sex

Farm work association[a]	Sex		Total
	Male	Female	
FO–FO	5.6 (n = 17)	—	5.6 (n = 17)
FW–FW	4.5 (n = 28)	4.7 (n = 3)	4.4 (n = 31)
FW–NFWA	1.6 (n = 11)	b	1.5 (n = 12)
NFWA–NFWA	3.9 (n = 80)	2.1 (n = 5)	3.8 (n = 85)
Total	4.1 (n = 140)	2.7 (n = 9)	4.0 (n = 149)

[a] An explanation of the farm work association symbols appears on p. 136.
[b] This cell contains only one employee.

Female plant employees in Scarriff expected lower alternative earnings than did male plant employees, though they also exhibited more variability by farm work association in their expectations than occurred in their present earnings.

In comparing the two areas in this respect, it is interesting to note that the mean alternative earnings expected by male plant employees who had no farm work association at any time in Scarriff was £1 higher than that of the corresponding employees in Tubbercurry. Similarly, farm operators in Scarriff expected higher alternative local earnings than did their Tubbercurry counterparts.

This is in contrast with the current situation of those two groups, who, as noted earlier, are currently receiving higher wages in Tubbercurry than in Scarriff. It is possible, therefore, to infer that industrialization has had relatively greater effect on income earning opportunities in the Tubbercurry area than in the Scarriff area in terms of differences between male plant employees' actual present wages and their expectations of alternative local earnings in the absence of the new plants.

In the case of female plant employees, there was little difference between the expected local alternative earnings in the two areas. Female employees in Tubbercurry had a mean expectation of £2.5, while those in Scarriff had a mean expectation of £2.7.

Finally, it is of interest to note that 10 of the Tubbercurry employees (6.3 per cent) felt that they could earn more locally in the absence of the plant than what they were currently receiving. Most of these were apprentices who were currently accepting lower wages during their apprenticeship than what they could have earned had they not become apprentices. A further 11 employees felt that in the absence of the plant they could earn the same as they were currently receiving, but the vast majority, 136 (or 86.6 per cent) felt that they could earn less in the local area than they were currently earning at the new plant.

Five of the Scarriff employees felt that they would be earning more in the AOI in the absence of the plant than the amount which they were currently receiving. One of these was an apprentice. The other 4 employees said that in the absence of the plant they would have been working at higher paying jobs in the area. However, these alternative jobs would have involved working harder or else working out of doors under unfavourable climatic conditions. Hence, these employees, because of the nature of the employment which they were offered at the plant, accepted lower wages in the plant than the wages which they would be receiving in the jobs which they would have had to accept, had not the plant been in Scarriff. Seven of the Scarriff employees felt that they could earn the same wages in the area in the absence of the plant. However, 92 per cent of those interviewed felt that in the absence of the plant, their alternative earnings in the Scarriff area would have been less than the amount currently being earned at the plant.

<h3 style="text-align:center">C. ALTERNATIVE EARNINGS ELSEWHERE</h3>

All plant employees who indicated that they would not have remained at work or come to work in the two areas were asked to estimate the weekly earnings which they felt they would have been obtaining currently in the places to which they would have gone for employment. Table 45 shows the distribution of these employees by their estimated alternative earnings elsewhere.

TABLE 45. Distribution of plant employees who would have left the areas by expected alternative earnings elsewhere

Weekly earnings (£) expected elsewhere	Tubbercurry		Scariff	
	Number	Per cent	Number	Per cent
Under 4	6	5.8	2	2.1
4 and under 8	9	8.7	5	5.2
8 and under 12	15	14.4	15	15.6
12 and under 16	15	14.4	25	26.0
16 and under 20	11	10.6	12	12.5
20 and under 24	18	17.3	16	16.7
24 and under 28	18	17.3	11	11.5
28 and over	12	11.5	10	10.4
Subtotal	104	100.0	96	100.0
No information	10	—	7	—
Other employees	43	—	48	—
Total	157	—	151	—

71 per cent of the Tubbercurry employees who would have gone to work elsewhere felt that they would have earned £12 or more per week in their new locations, while 77 per cent of those Scarriff employees who would have gone to work elsewhere felt they would have been earning £12 or more per week. However, more Tubbercurry employees felt they could have earned £20 or over elsewhere, 46 per cent as against 38 per cent of the Scarriff employees who would have gone elsewhere. Thus, more of the Scarriff employees who would have gone elsewhere had earnings expectations between £12 and £20. This fact is largely explained by skill differences among the two groups of employees and the fact that more of the employees who would have left the Tubbercurry area would have gone to England, where they would have obtained higher wages than in Ireland.

The mean alternative earnings expected elsewhere by plant employees who would have gone to work elsewhere are shown for the two areas in tables 46 and 47, classified by farm work association and by sex. The mean weekly earnings expected elsewhere by Tubbercurry employees (£18.2) was about £1 higher than the mean expected by Scarriff employees (£17.3). Both male and

TABLE 46. Mean alternative weekly earnings (£) expected elsewhere by Tubbercurry plant employees who would have gone to work elsewhere classified by farm work association and by sex

Farm work association[a]	Sex		Total
	Male	Female	
FO–FO	28.4 (n = 8)	—	28.4 (n = 8)
FW–FW	18.4 (n = 19)	8.3 (n = 8)	15.4 (n = 27)
FW–NFWA	15.7 (n = 5)	b	14.7 (n = 6)
NFWA–NFWA	20.1 (n = 46)	10.5 (n = 13)	18.0 (n = 59)
Total	20.4 (n = 82)	9.7 (n = 22)	18.2 (n = 104)

[a] An explanation of the farm work association symbols appears on p. 136.
[b] This cell contains only one employee.

TABLE 47. Mean alternative weekly earnings (£) expected elsewhere by Scarriff plant employees who would have gone to work elsewhere classified by farm work association and by sex

Farm work association[a]	Sex		Total
	Male	Female	
FO–FO	13.2 (n = 5)	—	13.2 (n = 5)
FW–FW	20.4 (n = 14)	9.0 (n = 2)	18.9 (n = 16)
FW–NFWA	17.2 (n = 10)	b	17.2 (n = 11)
NFWA–NFWA	18.5 (n = 59)	8.7 (n = 5)	17.7 (n = 64)
Total	18.3 (n = 91)	8.8 (n = 8)	17.3 (n = 99)

[a] An explanation of the farm work association symbols appears on p. 136.
[b] This cell contains only one employee.

female plant employees who would have left the Tubbercurry area had higher earnings expectations elsewhere than had the Scarriff employees, the differences being about £2 for male employees and about £1 for female employees.

The most striking difference between the two areas is the fact that farm operators who would have left the Tubbercurry area had a mean weekly earnings expectation of £28.4, the highest for any farm association group in Tubbercurry, while farm operators who would have left the Scarriff area had a mean weekly earnings expectation of £13.2, the lowest for any farm work association group in that area. Two possible explanations of this difference may be noted. Firstly, farm operators employed at the new plants had differing educational levels in the two areas. The mean number of years of post-primary education received by farm operator plant employees in Tubbercurry was 1.47 years, while that of their Scarriff counterparts was 0.30 years. Secondly, three fourths of the Tubbercurry farm operator plant employees who would have left the area would have gone to England, whereas none of those who would have left the Scarriff area indicated that he would have gone farther afield than to an adjoining county.

It is now possible to construct a measure of the non-income considerations which entered into the decision of those people, who would have sought employment elsewhere in the absence of the new plants, to accept employment at those plants rather than to seek employment elsewhere. Such a measure may be constructed by comparing, for this group of people, their expected earnings elsewhere with their actual current earnings at the new plants.

It matters not that these earnings expectations might not have been realized elsewhere. In fact, whether or not the expectations are realistic is irrelevant in the present context. The important consideration is that each of these individuals may be presumed to have compared this expectation with his current earnings at local industrial employment and, on the basis of such a comparison, decided to remain at work in the local plant. The difference between that expectation and his current plant earnings may, then, be used as a measure of the importance of whatever non-income considerations entered into his decision to work at the local industrial plant.

Tables 48 and 49 show, for the two areas, the mean difference between expected weekly earnings elsewhere and present earnings at the new plant for plant employees who would have left these areas in the absence of the new plants, classified by farm work association and by sex.

TABLE 48. Mean difference between present weekly earnings and alternative weekly earnings (£) expected elsewhere by Tubbercurry plant employees who would have gone to work elsewhere classified by farm work association and by sex[a]

| Farm work association[b] | Sex | | Total |
	Male	Female	
FO–FO	16.4 (n = 8)	—	16.4 (n = 4)
FW–FW	10.3 (n = 19)	3.0 (n = 8)	8.2 (n = 27)
FW–NFWA	−0.2 (n = 5)	c	0.6 (n = 6)
NFWA–NFWA	7.1 (n = 46)	4.5 (n = 13)	6.6 (n = 59)
Total	7.8 (n = 82)	3.9 (n = 22)	7.1 (n = 104)

[a] Difference is expressed as (alternative earnings—present earnings).
[b] An explanation of the farm work association symbols appears on p. 136.
[c] This cell contains only one employee.

TABLE 49. Mean difference between present weekly earnings and alternative weekly earnings (£) expected elsewhere by Scarriff plant employees who would have gone to work elsewhere classified by farm work association and by sex[a]

| Farm work association[b] | Sex | | Total |
	Male	Female	
FO–FO	3.0 (n = 5)	—	3.0 (n = 5)
FW–FW	10.7 (n = 14)	1.8 (n = 2)	9.5 (n = 16)
FW–NFWA	6.4 (n = 10)	c	6.4 (n = 11)
NFWA–NFWA	4.2 (n = 59)	1.1 (n = 5)	4.0 (n = 64)
Total	6.6 (n = 91)	1.3 (n = 7)	6.0 (n = 98)

[a] Difference is expressed as (alternative earnings—present earnings).
[b] An explanation of the farm work symbols appears on p. 136.
[c] This cell contains only one employee association.

As noted in table 48, the 104 Tubbercurry plant employees who indicated that they would have gone to work elsewhere in the absence of the new plants at Tubbercurry were currently receiving a mean of £7.1 less per week than the alternative earnings which they felt they would have been obtaining had they gone elsewhere. The corresponding figure for the 103 Scarriff employees who would have gone to work elsewhere was £6, as shown in table 49. It may thus be argued that other considerations besides the income available from plant employment and the alternative income available elsewhere entered into the decision-making process employed by those individuals in deciding to accept employment at the new plants.

A mean difference of £16.4 was reported by farm operators in Tubbercurry. This may be compared with a mean difference of £10.3 reported by the male non-operator farm worker group who did not change their farm work association. However, those male non-operator farm workers in Tubbercurry who ceased to have a farm work association reported no difference. Male plant employees who had no farm work association reported a difference of £7.8 per week.

It is to be expected that farm income considerations would be of importance to farm operators. Family farm income of those operators with plant employment in the Tubbercurry area was £3.8 per week, so if allowance is made for this item, the difference occurring in the case of the Tubbercurry farm operator plant employees becomes £12.6, about £2 higher than that reported by the male non-operator farm workers. Both groups reported a greater difference than did those employees who had no farm work association, indicating that those employees who had farming associations were prepared to make a greater income sacrifice in order to work in the Tubbercurry plant than were the employees who did not have any farming association.

In Scarriff, however, the farm operators employed at the plant reported a mean difference of £3, the smallest for any farm work association group. It will be recollected that these people had relatively low expectations regarding the alternative incomes which they would have been receiving elsewhere had they left the Scarriff AOI. When one bears in mind that the mean family farm income for this group was £5.9 per week, it is seen that farm operator plant employees in Scarriff did not feel that they could have obtained as high an income elsewhere as their present combined incomes from farming and plant employment. It was noted earlier that farm operator plant employees in Scarriff had relatively low expectations regarding their income earning ability elsewhere.

As was noted in the case of Tubbercurry, the male Scarriff plant employees who were non-operator farm workers and who did not subsequently change their farm work association reported a mean difference of £10.7 per week, while those male employees with no farm work association reported a mean difference of £4.2 per week. Thus, in both areas, non-operator farm workers reported a greater mean difference between their present plant earnings and the amount they felt they could earn had they gone to work elsewhere. Farm operator plant employees in Tubbercurry reported an even greater difference (after allowing for farm income) between present earnings and expected alternative earnings elsewhere.

D. HOUSEHOLD INCOME EFFECTS

All plant employees were asked whether their plant employment had given rise to an increase in their net household income, that is, after allowing for any costs which might have been involved in their present employment. As shown in table 50, 81 per cent of the Tubbercurry employees and 74 per cent of the Scarriff

TABLE 50. Distribution of plant employees by whether or not an increase in household income occurred as a result of their obtaining plant employment

	Tubbercurry		Scarriff	
	Number	Per cent	Number	Per cent
Increase reported	127	81.4	109	74.1
No increase reported	29	18.6	38	25.9
Subtotal	156	100.0	147	100.0
No information	1	—	4	—
Total	157	—	151	—

employees reported a net increase in household income as a result of obtaining employment at the new plants. Practically all of those reporting no increase had returned from abroad, for family or other reasons, to work in the plant. Others had been employed at different jobs prior to obtaining employment at the new plants. In each area, all but one of the farm operators who were employed at the plant reported an increase in household income.

The reported increments in household income ranged from less than £50 per year to more than £550 per year. The distribution of plant employees by amount of net increase in household income is shown in table 51. In both areas, the most frequently occurring increment reported was between £200 and £250 per

TABLE 51. Distribution of plant employees by amount of added annual household income reported as a result of obtaining plant employment

Amount of increase in income (£)	Tubbercurry		Scarriff	
	Number	Per cent	Number	Per cent
1– 49	6	5.2	6	5.7
50– 99	15	12.9	13	12.4
100–149	15	12.9	14	13.3
150–199	17	14.6	11	10.5
200–249	22	19.0	16	15.2
250–299	13	11.2	12	11.4
300–349	9	7.8	12	11.4
350–399	5	4.3	5	4.8
400–449	7	6.0	7	6.7
450–499	1	0.9	5	4.8
500–549	3	2.6	4	3.8
550 and over	3	2.6	—	—
Subtotal	116	100.0	105	100.0
No information on amount of increase	11	—	4	—
Did not report an increase	29	—	38	—
No information on whether or not an increase occurred	1	—	4	—
Total	157	—	151	—

year. Similarly, in both areas about 70 per cent of the increments were greater than £150 per year. All the increments reported by the Scarriff employees were less than £550 per year, while 3 Tubbercurry employees reported increments of £550 or more.

Table 52 shows the mean increments to household income reported by plant employees in each area, classified by farm

TABLE 52. Mean net increment to household annual income (£) reported by plant employees classified by farm work association[a]

Farm work association[b]	Tubbercurry	Scarriff
FO–FO	353 (n = 14)	285 (n = 15)
FW–FW	213 (n = 34)	233 (n = 25)
FW–NFWA	228 (n = 14)	203 (n = 9)
NFWA–NFWA	198 (n = 51)	233 (n = 52)
Total	225 (n = 116)	237 (n = 105)

[a] This table refers only to those employees reporting positive increments to household income.

[b] An explanation of the farm work association symbols appears on p. 136.

work association. These data refer to those employees who reported positive increments. The mean increment reported in Scarriff was £237, which was £12 higher than the mean increment of £225 reported in Tubbercurry. In both areas, farm operators reported substantially greater increments than did employees who had no farm work association, the difference between these two groups being greater in Tubbercurry (£155) than in Scarriff (£52). There was more variability among farm work association groups in Tubbercurry than in Scarriff regarding the amount of added household income which resulted from plant employment.

Male employees in Scarriff reported a mean increment of £243, while males in Tubbercurry reported a mean increment of £237 per year. On the other hand, female employees in Tubbercurry reported a mean increment of £200, while females in Scarriff reported a mean increment of £150 per year.

The aggregate of the positive increments to annual household income reported by the plant employees interviewed in

Tubbercurry was £28,950. The corresponding aggregate of the increments reported by the plant employees interviewed in Scarriff was £26,675. The distribution of these aggregate increments to annual household income of plant employees, classified by distance of residence from the plants, is shown in table 53. 56 per cent of the aggregate increment to household

TABLE 53. Distribution of aggregate increased annual household income (£) by distance of employees' residence from plant[a]

Distance from plant (miles)	Tubbercurry		Scarriff	
	Amount	Per cent	Amount	Per cent
Under 4	16,325	56.4	12,575	47.1
4 and under 8	6,675	23.0	6,875	25.8
8 and under 12	2,975	10.3	6,225	23.3
12 and under 16	1,875	6.5	875	3.3
16 and under 20	375	1.3	125	0.5
20 and over	725	2.5	—	—
Total	28,950	100.0	26,675	100.0

[a] This table refers only to plant employees who reported positive increments to household income.

income in the Tubbercurry area accrued to households within 4 miles of the plant, compared with 47 per cent of the aggregate increment in the Scarriff area accruing to households within 4 miles of that plant.

In the Tubbercurry area, the aggregate increment to household incomes declined steadily as distance from the plant increased. In Scarriff, on the other hand, the proportion of the aggregate increment to household income accruing to households located between 8 and 12 miles distant from the plant (23.3 per cent) was only slightly less than the proportion accruing to households which were between 4 and 8 miles distant from the plant. This is a consequence of the relatively high proportion of Scarriff plant employees who resided between 8 and 12 miles distant from the plant.

About 90 per cent of the aggregate increment to household incomes in the Tubbercurry area accrued to households located within a 12-mile radius of Tubbercurry. In Scarriff, over 95 per cent of the aggregate increment accrued to households located within 12 miles from the plant.

I I

Expenditure Effects

The expenditure effects arising from the increased income of households in both areas as a result of plant employment are analysed in the present chapter, which contains two sections. In section A, the allocation of the increased income among various expenditure categories is discussed, while section B contains an evaluation of the spatial incidence of these expenditure effects and an examination of spatial shifts in shopping patterns induced by industrialization.

A.   EXPENDITURE EFFECTS

All employees who had reported an increase in net household income as a result of industrial employment were asked to allocate the actual or planned use of this increase among a number of expenditure categories (including savings). Within the context of the present discussion, the term "savings" is to be understood as comprising money which was being accumulated and hoarded by plant employees, probably in bank accounts or post office savings accounts, and in respect of which no decision had been made regarding its future use. Some employees (13 in Tubbercurry and 6 in Scarriff) were unable, as shown in table 54, to give any information regarding the use to which the increment in their household income had been or was about to be put.

About 65 per cent of the employees who gave information regarding expenditures provided either percentage or actual allocations among the expenditure categories. About 26 per cent

153

TABLE 54. Distribution of plant employees by type of information given regarding expenditure of increase in household income

Type of information	Tubbercurry		Scarriff	
	Number	Per cent	Number	Per cent
Percentage	61	53.5	59	57.3
Pounds sterling	12	10.5	8	7.8
Rank	30	26.3	27	26.2
Tick (check)	11	9.7	9	8.7
Subtotal	114	100.0	103	100.0
No information on expenditure	13	—	6	—
Did not report an increase in income	29	—	38	—
No information on whether an increase in income occurred	1	—	4	—
Total	157	—	151	—

of the employees in each area made a ranking of the expenditure categories, while 11 Tubbercurry and 9 Scarriff employees indicated with a tick (check) that they had devoted some of the increased income to certain of the categories. It is thus possible to analyse the expenditure effects at three levels, viz. numbers mentioning each category, numbers giving various rankings to each category and, finally, amounts expended on each category.

1. Expenditure catagories mentioned

Table 55 contains a distribution of the various expenditure categories by the number of employees who mentioned each. In both areas, the two most frequently mentioned expenditure categories were savings and general living expenses, the former being more prevalent in Tubbercurry, where nearly half of those reporting devoted some of the increased income to savings, as opposed to one third of the Scarriff employees who reported on expenditures.

About a quarter of those reporting in each area said that some of the increased household income had been used to purchase household equipment. 30 per cent of the Tubbercurry group and

TABLE 55. Distribution of expenditure categories by number and per cent of plant employees mentioning each category

Expenditure category	Tubbercurry		Scarriff	
	Number	Per cent (n = 114)	Number	Per cent (n = 103)
Purchase household equipment	29	25.4	28	27.2
Purchase car	35	30.7	26	25.2
Purchase clothing	43	37.7	29	28.2
Educational expenses	11	9.6	10	9.7
Savings	54	47.4	35	34.0
Pay bills or repay loans	1	0.9	4	3.9
General living expenses	48	42.1	37	35.9
Entertainment	33	28.9	13	12.6
Purchase farm equipment or livestock	17	15.0	20	19.4
Purchase or improve land	2	1.8	5	4.9
Purchase or improve house	—	—	4	3.9
Invested in own non-farm business	2	1.8	—	—
Given or sent to relatives	1	0.9	1	1.0
Other	2	1.8	2	1.9

25 per cent of the Scarriff group had used some of the increase to purchase a car. Nearly 38 per cent of the Tubbercurry employees reported some expenditure on clothing, while 28 per cent of the Scarriff employees did so. This reflects the higher proportion of female employees in Tubbercurry. The other major difference between the two areas, that involving expenditure on entertainment (29 per cent in Tubbercurry and 13 per cent in Scarriff) largely arose because of the greater number of younger, unmarried employees in Tubbercurry.

About 10 per cent in each area used some of the increase for educational expenses. The number using the added income to repay debts was quite small in each area, being 4 in Scarriff and 1 in Tubbercurry. Farm investment uses were reported by a somewhat higher proportion of the Scarriff employees. Farm investment uses were not reported exclusively by farm operators; some non-operator farm workers reported that some of their added income was used for farm investment on their home farms.

Four Scarriff employees reported an investment in housing, while none of those reporting in Tubbercurry did so.

2. Ranking of expenditure categories

The number of employees who provided rankings of the expenditure categories (or actual or percentage expenditures from which rankings could be derived) was 103 in Tubbercurry and 94 in Scarriff. The expenditure categories are distributed in table 56 by the number of plant employees who gave first (or joint first)

TABLE 56. Distribution of expenditure categories by number of plant employees attaching first (or joint first) ranking to each category

Expenditure category	Tubbercurry		Scarriff	
	Number	Per cent (n = 103)	Number	Per cent (n = 94)
Purchase household equipment	10	9.7	12	12.8
Purchase car	15	14.6	11	11.7
Purchase clothing	7	6.8	6	6.4
Educational expenses	5	4.8	3	3.2
Savings	21	20.4	13	13.8
Pay bills or repay loans	—	—	4	4.3
General living expenses	38	36.9	25	26.6
Entertainment	14	13.6	5	5.3
Purchase farm equipment or livestock	8	7.8	16	17.0
Purchase or improve land	1	1.0	3	3.2
Purchase or improve house	—	—	4	4.3
Invested in own non-farm business	1	1.0	—	—
Given or sent to relatives	—	—	1	1.1
Other	1	1.0	—	—

rank to each category. Thus the total number of rankings shown for each area in table 57 exceeds the number of employees providing such rankings to the degree that some employees provided joint rankings.

37 per cent of the Tubbercurry employees and 27 per cent of the Scarriff employees reporting attached first (or joint first) rank to general living expenses. This category, in both areas, was

TABLE 57. Mean annual expenditure ($\mathcal{L}$) on various expenditure categories from increased household income of Tubbercurry plant employees classified by farm work association

Expenditure category	Farm work association[a]					Total
	FO–FO	FW–FW	FW–NFWA	NFWA–NFWA		
Household equipment	82.6	6.0	—	13.5		17.1
Car	53.8	31.8	25.4	32.7		33.3
Clothing	9.4	18.2	19.5	29.5		22.5
Educational expenses	—	—	8.1	1.2		1.7
Savings	33.5	49.0	51.6	33.4		41.3
Pay bills or repay loan	—	—	—	—		—
General living expenses	60.0	53.2	62.2	57.0		56.0
Entertainment	—	13.7	43.4	45.1		30.9
Farm equipment or livestock	77.0	11.3	—	—		11.6
Land purchase or improvement	56.9	—	—	—		6.3
Housing	—	—	—	—		—
Invested in non-farm business	—	11.8	—	—		3.1
Given or sent to relatives	—	—	—	—		—
Other uses	—	2.1	—	0.1		0.6

[a] An explanation of the farm work association symbols appears on p. 136.

TABLE 58. Mean annual expenditure ($£$) on various expenditure categories from increased household income of Scarriff plant employees classified by farm work association

Expenditure category	Farm work association[a]				Total
	FO–FO	FW–FW	FW–NFWA	NFWA–NFWA	
Household equipment	—	3.6	—	19.6	10.6
Car	—	35.4	—	15.7	17.9
Clothing	—	17.7	—	23.4	16.9
Educational expenses	—	—	5.0	3.2	3.4
Savings	—	35.3	55.0	25.2	22.3
Pay bills or repay loan	—	66.4	95.0	23.5	15.7
General living expenses	30.4	27.2	—	91.9	74.6
Entertainment	—	8.3	50.0	15.1	14.8
Farm equipment or livestock	106.5	12.2	—	—	23.0
Land purchase or improvement	114.3	21.9	—	—	15.2
Housing	30.3	—	—	3.8	14.0
Invested in non-farm business	—	12.5	—	—	—
Given or sent to relatives	—	3.8	—	—	3.4
Other uses	15.0			4.3	4.8

[a] An explanation of the farm work association symbols appears on p. 136.

ranked first (or joint first) by a substantially greater proportion
of employees than was any other expenditure category. Farm
investment expenditures received the second largest number of
first (or joint first) rankings in Scarriff, followed by savings and
household equipment. In Tubbercurry, on the other hand, savings
received the second largest number of first (or joint first) rankings,
followed by car purchase and entertainment expenses.

Each of the four Scarriff employees who indicated that they
spent some of their increased household income in buying or
improving their houses attached a first (or joint first) ranking to
this expenditure. Similarly, 3 Scarriff employees attached a first
(or joint first) ranking to the purchase or improvement of farm
land, while only one Tubbercurry employee did so. It would thus
appear that more of the Scarriff employees devoted major
portions of increased household income to investment activities
than did the Tubbercurry employees, for whom savings and
immediate consumption expenditures played a greater role. The
definition of savings as used in the present chapter will be recalled
at this point. Use of the words savings and investment in the
present chapter is not to be construed in terms of macroeconomic
savings-investment equilibria.

3. Expenditure on each category

73 employees in Tubbercurry and 67 employees in Scarriff provided either a percentage or actual allocation of their increased
household income among the expenditure categories. Since the
increments in household income were known in the case of all
the employees who gave a percentage allocation among expenditure categories, it was possible to compute actual allocations
therefrom.

Tables 57 and 58 show the mean expenditures per annum
from the increased household income reported by plant employees
in both areas, classified by farm work association. Since some
farm work association groups of plant employees had only one
person reporting on the allocation of increased income among

expenditure categories, data in respect of such groups are not presented in tables 57 and 58. However, the information supplied by those employees was included in computing mean expenditure on each expenditure category for all employees reporting.

In both areas, mean expenditure on general living expenses was higher than on any other expenditure category. In Tubbercurry, the next three categories in order of importance were savings, car expenses and entertainment, while the corresponding categories in Scarriff were farm equipment or livestock, savings and car expenses.

Plant employees who had no farm work association, either before or subsequent to plant employment, devoted more of their increased household income to general living expenses than to any other expenditure category. This was so in both areas. However, among the Tubbercurry group the second expenditure category in order of importance was entertainment expenditure, while in Scarriff entertainment expenditures were ranked seventh by this group of employees. The Scarriff group tended to devote approximately equal amounts to savings, getting out of debt and to expenditure on clothing, which were next in order of importance to general living expenses.

Farm operators in both areas allocated none of the increased income to entertainment expenditures. Allocations to investment uses such as purchases of farm equipment and livestock and acquisition or improvement of land outweighed the amount used for general living expenses. Farm operators in the Tubbercurry area made substantial purchases of household equipment from the added income while those in the Scarriff area devoted as much to improvement of their housing facilities as they did to general living expenses.

These data regarding expenditures support the hypothesis that increased household incomes arising directly from industrialization gave rise to increased expenditures on good and services on the part of households experiencing such increased incomes. Such expenditures were on consumer goods, entertainment and other services and on farm investment goods, thus providing increased demand for these goods and services which would give rise to indirect effects on businesses providing these services.

B. SPATIAL INCIDENCE OF EXPENDITURE EFFECTS

All plant employees who reported an increase in household income as a result of plant employment (except those employees who reported that all of the increased income had been saved) were asked to indicate the town in which the increased income was mainly spent. Some employees in each area reported that the extra income had been spent in roughly equal proportions in more than one town, but the bulk of the employees mentioned just one town.

The towns mentioned in this regard by the Tubbercurry employees are shown in table 59. The total number of responses was 122. The town of Tubbercurry was mentioned 76 times,

TABLE 59. Distribution of towns by number of times mentioned by Tubbercurry plant employees as the main spending location of increased household income

Town	Times Mentioned	Per cent of Mentions (n = 122)
Within the AOI		
Tubbercurry	76	62.3
Ballymote	8	6.6
Charlestown	8	6.6
Aclare	1	0.8
Coolaney	1	0.8
Outside the AOI		
Swinford	2	1.6
Ballina (Mayo)	2	1.6
Sligo	21	17.2
Other towns	3	2.5

thus receiving 62 per cent of all mentions. Ballymote and Charlestown were each mentioned 8 times. Towns outside the Tubbercurry AOI were mentioned on 28 occasions as being the places wherein plant employees spent most of their increased household income.

Chief among these towns was Sligo, the county seat, which had a 1966 population of 13,424 people and is situated about 25 miles distance from Tubbercurry.

Nearly all of the employees residing in the Tubbercurry DED and the adjoining DEDs mentioned the town of Tubbercurry. Those mentioning Ballymote and Charlestown were all residents of these towns or of the adjoining DEDs. Plant employees who mentioned Sligo resided in many of the DEDs, though more of them resided to the north of Tubbercurry than to the south of Tubbercurry. It is of interest to note that 6 residents of the Tubbercurry DED mentioned the town of Sligo. Five of these were either non-heads of households or else resided in one person households.

Similar information regarding the Scarriff employees is shown in table 60. The town of Scarriff was mentioned 46 times,

TABLE 60. Distribution of towns by number of times mentioned by Scarriff plant employees as the main spending location of increased household income

Town	Times Mentioned	Per cent of Mentions (n = 95)
Within the AOI		
Scarriff	46	48.4
Mountshannon	2	2.1
Feakle	4	4.2
Whitegate	2	2.1
Broadford	2	2.1
Killaloe	9	9.5
Bodyke	1	1.1
Outside the AOI		
Ennis	2	2.1
Limerick	19	20.0
Ballina (Tipperary)	2	2.1
Other towns	6	6.3

receiving nearly half of all mentions. All other towns in the Scarriff AOI were mentioned infrequently except Killaloe which was mentioned 9 times. Over 30 per cent of the towns mentioned were outside the Scarriff AOI. The most frequently mentioned town outside the AOI was Limerick (mentioned 19 times) which had a 1966 population of 55,912 and is situated about 25 miles distance from Scarriff.

In comparing the spatial incidence of the direct expenditure effects in the two areas, it is evident that the proportion of plant employees who spent the major part of their increased household income in the town wherein the new plant was situated was greater among the Tubbercurry employees than among the Scarriff employees. The town of Tubbercurry received over 62 per cent of the mentions among the Tubbercurry employees, while the town of Scarriff received 48 per cent of the mentions among the Scarriff employees. Apparently, therefore, the expenditure effects of industrialization were more concentrated in the town of Tubbercurry than in the town of Scarriff.

This difference was to be expected on the basis of the greater number of Scarriff employees who resided in DEDs containing other towns within the areas. For example, most of the plant employees who resided in Killaloe spent most of their increased income in Killaloe.

It is also apparent that there were substantial leakages of the increased household income from both areas through expenditures made outside the areas. About 20 per cent of the employees who had received increased household income in each area reported that this increased income was mainly spent in a large town situated about 25 miles distance from the town in which the plant was located.

Further evidence to support the proposition that a relatively greater expenditure effect was manifested on the town of Tubbercurry than on the town of Scarriff is provided by the fact that 109 of the Tubbercurry employees (70 per cent) reported an increase in shopping in Tubbercurry town as a result of their plant employment, while 89 of the Scarriff employees (less than 60 per cent) reported an increase in shopping in Scarriff town as a result of their plant employment.

Of the employees who reported an increase in shopping in Tubbercurry, about half indicated that they had reduced shopping in other towns. Nearly two thirds of the corresponding Scarriff employees reduced their shopping in other towns. Of course, many of these employees were people who had moved into the AOIs in association with their plant employment. Hence, the towns in which these people decreased their shopping were distributed over a wide geographical area.

However, as shown in tables 61 and 62, other towns within the two AOIs experienced a decrease in shopping by plant

TABLE 61. Distribution of towns in the Tubbercurry AOI by number of plant employees who decreased shopping in each town and increased shopping in Tubbercurry as a result of obtaining plant employment

Town	Employees	
	Number	Per cent (n = 56)
Ballymote	12	21.4
Curry	3	5.4
Charlestown	9	16.1
Coolaney	1	1.8

TABLE 62. Distribution of towns in the Scarriff AOI by number of plant employees who decreased shopping in each town and increased shopping in Scarriff as a result of obtaining plant employment

Town	Employees	
	Number	Per cent (n = 57)
Mountshannon	2	3.5
Feakle	3	5.3
Whitegate	2	3.5
Broadford	3	5.3
Killaloe	10	17.5

employees who increased their shopping in Tubbercurry and in Scarriff. In the Tubbercurry area the towns of Ballymote and Charlestown exhibited the greatest decrease in shopping as a result of the Tubbercurry industrialization, while in the Scarriff area the town of Killaloe experienced a corresponding decrease in shopping as a result of the Scarriff industrialization.

There was thus a shift in the location of shopping by families of plant employees as a result of obtaining industrial employment in Tubbercurry and in Scarriff. In both cases the shift involved a decrease in shopping by plant employees in other towns in the AOI and an increase in shopping in the town wherein the plant was situated. In both areas, practically all plant employees who reported shopping shifts from other towns to the plant town were residents of the DEDs containing these other towns or of the DEDs adjoining these DEDs.

However, the shift in shopping location involved some goods and services to a greater extent than others, as shown in table 63. Groceries and clothing were involved much more frequently in

TABLE 63. Distribution of goods and services by number of times mentioned as being involved in the shift in shopping patterns by plant employees who increased shopping in Tubbercurry and Scarriff and decreased shopping in other towns as a result of obtaining plant employment

| Item | Employees mentioning each item | | | |
| | Tubbercurry | | Scarriff | |
	Number	Per cent (n = 56)	Number	Per cent (n = 57)
Groceries	39	69.6	40	70.2
Clothing	37	66.1	41	71.9
Hardware	16	28.6	7	12.3
Drugs and cosmetics	14	25.0	12	21.1
Doctor or dental services	14	25.0	10	17.5
Entertainment	22	39.3	11	19.3
Petrol, oil, car repair	18	32.1	13	22.8
Newspapers and magazines	25	44.6	10	17.5
Furniture and household appliances	10	17.9	5	8.8

the shift in both areas than were other goods and services. About 70 per cent of the employees who increased shopping in Tubbercurry and Scarriff and decreased shopping in other towns indicated that groceries and clothing were involved in the shift. All other goods and services were involved in less than half of the shifts in each area.

All goods and services other than groceries and clothing were involved more frequently in shopping shifts in Tubbercurry than in Scarriff. In fact, newspapers and magazines were featured in 45 per cent of the Tubbercurry shifts, but in less than 20 per cent of the Scarriff shifts. In both areas, the items involved least frequently in shifts of shopping location were furniture and household appliances.

It is thus apparent that the indirect effects on local business firms arising from changes in the demand for goods and services differ considerably among business firms according to the goods and services in the provision of which they are engaged. Greater effects may be expected to be felt by grocery stores and clothiers than, say, by suppliers of furniture following industrialization in an area.

12

Farm Business Effects

The direct effects on their farm businesses following the plant employment of farm operators are discussed in this chapter. The discussion is confined to the effects observed on the farms of farm operators who did not change their farm work association subsequent to obtaining plant employment. Farm operators in this category numbered 15 in the Tubbercurry area and 17 in the Scarriff area.

The manner in which the nature and magnitude of these direct effects were determined has been discussed previously. Suffice it to remark, at this stage, that in respect of each farm business characteristic examined, the farm operators were asked to report any changes in that characteristic which had occurred as a direct result of their obtaining employment at the new plants.

For convenience of presentation, this chapter is organized as follows. The direct effects of plant employment on labour and machinery utilization are examined in section A. The direct effects on land utilization and livestock enterprises are discussed in sections B and C, which also contain a quantitative evaluation of the magnitude of these effects. Finally, section D contains an evaluation of the direct effects on the total farm output of those farms.

A. LABOUR AND MACHINERY

The effects of farm operator plant employment on the farm labour and machinery use on their farms is shown in tables 64 and 65. All farm operators employed in Tubbercurry reported a

167

TABLE 64. Effect of operator plant employment on farm labour and machinery use in the Tubbercurry area

Characteristic	Per cent reporting[a]		
	No change	Increase	Decrease
Amount of time spent by operator at farm work	—	—	100.0
Amount of time spent by operator's wife at farm work[b]	18.2	72.7	9.1
Amount of time spent by other family members at farm work[c]	40.0	50.0	10.0
Total amount of time spent by all family members at farm work	6.7	26.6	66.7
Amount of hired labour used	40.0	46.7	13.3
Amount of time spent working at turf production by operator	53.3	—	46.7
Use of own machinery and equipment	73.4	26.6	—
Use of hired machinery and equipment	46.7	46.7	6.6

[a] Except where noted otherwise, percentages refer to 15 farm operators.
[b] Percentages for this item refer to the 11 married farm operators.
[c] Percentages for this item refer to the 10 farms having other family members.

TABLE 65. Effect of operator plant employment on farm labour and machinery use in the Scarriff area

Characteristic	Per cent reporting[a]		
	No change	Increase	Decrease
Amount of time spent by operator at farm work	17.6	—	82.4
Amount of time spent by operator's wife at farm work[b]	63.6	36.4	—
Amount of time spent by other family members at farm work[c]	71.4	28.6	—
Total amount of time spent by all family members at farm work	35.3	5.9	58.8
Amount of hired labour used	64.7	23.5	11.8
Amount of time spent working at turf production by operator	76.5	—	23.5
Use of own machinery and equipment	70.6	17.6	11.8
Use of hired machinery and equipment	58.8	41.2	—

[a] Except where noted otherwise, percentages refer to 17 farm operators.
[b] Percentages for this item refer to the 11 married farm operators.
[c] Percentages for this item refer to the 14 farms having other family members.

decrease in the amount of time which they devoted to farm work. However, 17.6 per cent of the farm operators employed at the Scarriff plant reported no change in their farm work input as a result of plant employment.

It is to be expected that farm operators would probably decrease the amount of time spent at farm work as a result of obtaining plant employment. The fact that some reported no change requires an explanation. It is possible that these farm operators may have overlooked certain minor changes in the amount of time they devoted to farm work. It is more likely, however, that a substitution of work for leisure time occurred in the case of those farm operators, possibly through early rising or working late into evenings on their farms. It is also possible, of course, that the labour input of those farm operators was so low that their acceptance of plant employment largely involved utilization of what was formerly idle time. In such cases, there would be little adjustment pressure arising from loss of operator labour.

In Tubbercurry, nearly three-fourths of the wives of married farm operator plant employees increased the amount of time which they devoted to farm work, about twice as high as the proportion of wives who increased their farm work in Scarriff. Similarly, on 50 per cent of the Tubbercurry farms which had more family members than the operator and his wife the amount of farm work done by the other family members increased. Increased farm work by other family members occurred on less than one-third of the Scarriff farms where such family members were present.

Part of the explanation of this difference may lie in the fact that on some of the Scarriff farms there was no reduction in the amount of time devoted to farm work by the farm operator as a result of his obtaining plant employment. Hence, some of the Scarriff farms would have little need for labour or other substitution to occur.

However, it is also possible that the supply elasticity of family labour on some of the Scarriff farms was lower than on the

Tubbercurry farms. It will be recollected that the mean number of family members who did some farm work on the Tubbercurry farms was greater than on the Scarriff farms.

Some support for both of these possible explanations may be found in an examination of changes occurring in the total amount of time spent by all family members at farm work. On 35 per cent of the Scarriff farms, there was no change reported in this quantity, while no change occurred on only 6.7 per cent of the Tubbercurry farms. Changes in the labour inputs of wives and other family members would be normally expected to occur only when changes had occurred in the amount of labour input by the farm operators.

It may be expected, however, that the labour services of wives and other family members would not be perfect substitutes for farm operator labour. Hence, in order to effectively replace a loss of operator labour, it may be expected that the increase in amount of family labour would need to be greater than the loss of operator labour. In such cases, then, the effect on the total amount of family labour used would be an increase. On about one-fourth of the Tubbercurry farms an increase occurred in the total time spent at farm work by all family members.

This would indicate that family labour on those farms was not regarded as a perfect substitute for operator labour and also that the supply of this family labour was sufficiently elastic that it could be provided in greater absolute quantities than involved in the loss of operator labour.

On the Scarriff farms, on the other hand, only 6 per cent of farms reported an increase in total time devoted to farm work by all family members. This does not mean, however, that farm output would have been reduced on those farms as a result. Depending on the nature of any farm investment effects of increased household income arising from plant employment, the value of output might remain unchanged or actually increase even though the substitution effects were weak.

The proportion of farm operators reporting an increase in the amount of hired labour used was about twice as high in Tubbercurry as in Scarriff. This suggests that it was less possible to replace losses of operator labour with farm labour on the Tubbercurry farms than on the Scarriff farms, even though there were more increases reported in the use of family labour on the Tubbercurry farms than on the Scarriff farms. Further support for this view may be found in the fact that increased use of own machinery and equipment was reported on 26.6 per cent of the Tubbercurry farms, as opposed to 17.6 per cent of the Scarriff farms, while the proportion of farms on which the use of hired machinery and equipment was increased was also greater in Tubbercurry than in Scarriff.

The pervading feature of tables 64 and 65 is that in the case of all characteristics, save one, the proportion of Scarriff farm operators reporting no change was larger than the proportion of Tubbercurry farm operators reporting no change. This indicates that substitution effects following the loss of farm operator labour occurred more frequently on the Tubbercurry farms than on the Scarriff farms.

B. LAND UTILIZATION

Data regarding the direct effects of plant employment of farm operators on the land utilization patterns of their farms are

TABLE 66. Effects of operator plant employment on land utilization in the Tubbercurry area[a]

Characteristic	Per cent reporting[a]		
	No change	Increase	Decrease
Total area farmed	60.0	6.7	33.3
Land rented for grazing	73.3	6.7	20.0
Land rented for crops	73.3	—	26.7
Grain crops	33.3	—	66.7
Root and grain crops	46.7	—	53.3
Hay	73.3	20.0	6.7
Pasture	33.3	53.4	13.3

[a] Percentages refer to 15 farm operators.

TABLE 67. Effects of operator plant employment on land utilization in the Scarriff area

Characteristic	Per cent reporting[a]		
	No change	Increase	Decrease
Total area farmed	82.4	17.6	—
Land rented for grazing	88.2	5.9	5.9
Land rented for crops	94.1	—	5.9
Grain crops	52.9	—	47.1
Root and grain crops	64.7	5.9	29.4
Hay	64.7	23.5	11.8
Pasture	52.9	41.2	5.9

[a] Percentages refer to 17 farm operators.

presented in tables 66 and 67. A much higher proportion of the Tubbercurry farm operators reported that their plant employment had given rise to decreases in total area farmed, in land rented for grazing, in land rented for crops, in acreage of grain crops and in acreage of root and green crops sown. For each of these items, the proportion of operators reporting no change was much higher in Scarriff than in Tubbercurry.

In both areas, the most frequently occurring changes in land utilization involved decreases in grain crop acreage and in root and green crop acreage and increases in the acreage under hay and pasture. More increases in pasture than in hay were reported in each area. These changes are as might be expected on a priori grounds, since grain crops and root and green crops are considerably more labour intensive crop enterprises than are hay and pasture.

Once again, however, it is noted that the frequency of decreases caused in these labour-intensive crops was greater among the Tubbercurry farm operators who had plant employment than among the Scarriff farm operator plant employees. This observation is highly consistent with the evidence contained in the previous section which indicated that the loss of operator labour on farms where the operator had obtained plant employment had more serious implications for the farm businesses of those farms in the Tubbercurry area than in the Scarriff area.

It is interesting to note that 17.6 per cent of the Scarriff farm operator plant employees indicated that they had increased their total area farmed as a result of obtaining plant employment. It will be recollected that, during the discussion of expenditure effects in a previous chapter, it was noted that Scarriff farm operator plant employees devoted a relatively large portion of their increased income to the expenditure category which was labelled "land purchase or improvement". Apparently, those plant employee farm operators in the Scarriff area who invested in their farm businesses decided to invest at the extensive rather than at the intensive margin of production.

Further evidence to support this contention is provided by the data in table 68, which contains a quantitative assessment of

TABLE 68. Estimated magnitude of direct effects of farm operator plant employment on land utilization[a]

Characteristic (acres)	Tubbercurry		Scarriff	
	Total Change	Mean per farm (n = 15)	Total change	Mean per farm (n = 17)
Total area farmed	14.0	0.93	37.0	2.18
Land rented for grazing	19.0	1.27	−4.0	−0.24
Land rented for crops	−8.0	−0.53	−6.0	−0.35
Grain crops	−21.5	−1.43	−12.8	−0.75
Root and green crops	−11.3	−0.75	−9.2	−0.54
Hay	7.0	0.47	−1.5	−0.09
Pasture	39.8	2.65	58.5	3.44

[a] Positive cell entries indicate increases while negative cell entries indicate decreases.

the direct effects of farm operator plant employment on their farm businesses. It will be noted that the total area of land farmed by the 17 plant employee farm operators in Scarriff was increased by 37 acres as a direct effect induced by their plant employment. The aggregate level of all categories of land use except pasture declined for this group. Hence, all of the decreases reported in the other land utilization categories represented land which was switched to pasture. In addition, all of the new land acquired by this group of farm operators was also devoted to pasture.

Both in aggregate terms and in terms of mean per farm the decrease in the amount of land devoted to grain crops and to root and green crops was greater in Tubbercurry than in Scarriff. Corresponding to the decrease in crop acreage, both groups of farm operators reduced the amount of land which they had rented for crop production. However, in aggregate the Scarriff group of farm operators also reduced the amount of land rented for grazing and then purchased grazing land. On the other hand, in aggregate the Tubbercurry group of operators rented an additional 19 acres of land for grazing.

Thus, it is seen that both groups of farm operator plant employees transferred land from labour intensive to labour extensive uses, mainly grassland. In addition to this transfer, both groups acquired additional land, the Scarriff group by purchase, the Tubbercurry group by rental, which was also devoted to pasture.

C.   LIVESTOCK ENTERPRISES

Direct effects of operator plant employment on livestock enterprises are shown in tables 69 and 70. As might be expected on a priori grounds and in conjunction with the already observed increase in the acreage under grassland on their farms, about 30 per cent of the Scarriff farm operator plant employees increased their numbers of cattle, other than milch cows, as a result of obtaining plant employment.

The forces inducing this increase may be twofold. Since cattle-raising in association with grassland is a labour-extensive enterprise, there would be an incentive to reallocate farm resources

TABLE 69. Effects of operator plant employment on livestock enterprises in the Tubbercurry area.

Characteristic	Per cent reporting[a]		
	No change	Increase	Decrease
Cows	20.0	33.3	46.7
Other cattle	33.3	60.0	6.7
Ewes	86.7	—	13.3
Sows	80.0	—	20.0
Pigs reared	66.7	6.7	26.6
Turkeys reared	73.4	—	26.6
Ordinary fowl	66.7	—	33.3

[a] Percentages refer to 15 farm operators.

TABLE 70. Effects of operator plant employment on livestock enterprises in the Scarriff area

Characteristic	Per cent reporting[a]		
	No change	Increase	Decrease
Cows	94.1	—	5.9
Other cattle	70.6	29.4	—
Ewes	94.1	5.9	—
Sows	94.1	—	5.9
Pigs reared	82.3	5.9	11.8
Turkeys reared	94.1	—	5.9
Ordinary fowl	100.0	—	—

[a] Percentages refer to 17 farm operators.

towards the production of these items on farms where the loss of operator labour following plant employment was not replaceable by other family labour. In addition, the farm investment effect arising from increased household income provided by the non-farm employment may provide a ready means of effecting such a production shift.

Decreases in numbers of ewes and sows kept and in numbers of pigs and poultry reared were reported more frequently by farm operator plant employees in Tubbercurry than in Scarriff.

The changes which occurred in cow numbers are quite interesting. In Scarriff, 6 per cent of the farm operator plant employees reported a decrease in cow numbers, while 94 per cent reported no change. However, in the Tubbercurry area, about half of the farm operator plant employees reported that a decrease had occurred.

Since the keeping of milch cows is a more labour-intensive enterprise than the rearing of cattle on grassland, effects emanating from loss of operator labour through plant employment might be expected to induce decreases rather than increases in cow numbers. However, in the Tubbercurry area there has been some recent expansion in creamery milk production. Apparently for those farm operators who increased cow numbers as a result of obtaining plant employment, the farm investment effect arising from increased household income which enabled them to purchase those cows outweighed any influences which might have tended to reduce cow numbers as a result of loss of operator labour.

The aggregate and mean magnitude per farm of the direct effects of operator plant employment on farm livestock enterprises are shown in table 71.

TABLE 71. Estimated magnitude of direct effects of farm operator plant employment on livestock enterprises[a]

	Tubbercurry		Scarriff	
Characteristic (number)	Total Change	Mean per farm (n = 15)	Total Change	Mean per farm (n = 17)
Cows	3.0	0.20	−2.0	−0.12
Other cattle	26.0	1.73	36.0	2.12
Ewes	−8.0	−0.53	5.0	0.29
Sows	−6.0	−0.40	−1.0	−0.06
Pigs reared	−34.0	−2.27	1.0	0.06
Turkeys reared	−68.0	−4.53	−10.0	−0.59
Ordinary fowl	−140.0	−9.33	—	—

[a] Positive cell entries indicate increases while negative cell entries indicate decreases.

The most striking features of table 71 are that numbers of cattle, other than milch cows, were directly increased by 36 on farms of the Scarriff farm operator plant employees, a mean increase of 2.12 per farm and that numbers of other cattle were directly increased by 26 on farms of the Tubbercurry farm operator plant employees, a mean increase of 1.73 cattle per farm.

Also worthy of note is that the number of pigs per annum reared to bacon weight was reduced by 34 on the Tubbercurry group of farms, while the aggregate number of sows was reduced by 6. There were also sizeable reductions in numbers of poultry on the Tubbercurry farms.

The aggregate net increase of 3 cows shown in table 71 for the Tubbercurry group of farms masks the real situation, since a high proportion of these farm operators increased their cow numbers and a high proportion decreased cow numbers. The aggregate direct increase in cow numbers reported by those farm operators who increased cow numbers was 17. The aggregate direct decrease reported by those who decreased cow numbers was 14. Hence, an aggregate net increase of 3 cows results.

D. TOTAL FARM OUTPUT

The net effect of employment of a farm operator at an industrial plant on the total output of his farm depends on the relative importance of the substitution effects arising from loss of operator labour and the farm investment effects arising from increased household income obtained as a result of plant employment.

So far during the present discussion it has been apparent that substitution effects played a prominent role in the farm businesses of farm operators who obtained plant employment. The presence of investment effects has also been noted, for example, acquisition of cows by some of the Tubbercurry group, acquisition of other cattle by both groups and purchase of land by both groups.

It may be helpful at this point to recall that those farm operator plant employees in Scarriff who reported on the allocation of their increased income among expenditure categories reported mean annual expenditures of £114.3 on land purchase or improvement and £106.5 on purchase of farm equipment or livestock. The corresponding group of Tubbercurry employees reported mean expenditures of £56.9 on land purchase or improvement and £77 on purchase of farm equipment or livestock. Since the farms of farm operator plant employees in both areas had a low inventory value of farm machinery and equipment when the study was conducted it may be concluded that most of the investment effect designated as farm equipment or livestock was devoted to purchases of livestock.

As discussed in an earlier chapter, little effect on total farm output was expected on a priori grounds. There is no reason to believe that farm output would be decreased as a result of operator employment on the 17.6 per cent of Scarriff farm operator plant employee farms where, as noted earlier in the present chapter, the amount of time devoted to farm work by the farm operators did not decrease. In fact, it might well have been that some farm investment effects were present which would tend to raise output on those farms.

All of the farm operator plant employees were asked whether, in their own judgement, they would say that the value of output from their farms was increased, decreased or unchanged by the fact that they had come to work at the plant. In Scarriff, 47.1 per cent said that the value of their farm output had been increased as a result of their plant employment; a further 35.3 per cent said that it had been unchanged, while only 17.6 per cent said that the value of their farm output had fallen as a result of their plant employment.

Similarly, in Tubbercurry 40 per cent of farm operator plant employees reported an increase in the value of their farm output as a result of obtaining plant employment; 33.3 per cent reported no change, while only 26.7 per cent reported that a decrease in the value of their farm output had been caused by their plant employment.

All operators who did not report a decrease in value of farm output as a result of their plant employment were asked to explain how farm output remained unchanged or increased despite the fact that they had less time to devote to farm work following acceptance of plant employment. The explanations offered by the farm operators are of considerable interest.

Some of the explanations given for an increased value of farm output as a result of plant employment were: "We can live on factory income and put back farm profits into the farm", "can afford manure now with the extra money from the factory", "bought extra cattle", "more money, more manuring, so stock has increased", "more capital to put into the farm", "more fertilizer and more dry stock", etc. All of the replies from the farm operators who reported an increase in the value of farm output as a result of plant employment emphasize the crucial role played by the farm investment effect of increased household income obtained as a result of plant employment.

Most of the reasons given by farm operators who reported that the value of farm production was unchanged by their obtaining plant employment tended to emphasize the substitution effects. Some replies were: "Better managed now than it was", "worked harder and earlier rising", "employ casual labour", "sister does some farm work now". However, some of the replies also involved the farm investment effect, e.g. "can buy bag fertilizer now and carry more stock".

It may thus be concluded that strong farm investment effects occurred on many of the farms of operators who obtained employment at the new plants. Where these effects occurred, they tended to give rise to an increase in the value of farm output, as a result of the operator obtaining plant employment.

On other farms where the effects were mainly substitution effects, value of output tended to remain unchanged. Only on relatively few farms was the situation such that combined substitution and farm investment effects did not balance the effects emanating from the loss of operator labour.

Increases in the value of farm output may normally be expected to give rise to increases in farm income obtained from such farms, while decreases in the value of farm output may normally be expected to give rise to decreases in farm income. In cases of the latter type, one would expect that increases in non-farm income of farm operators as a result of obtaining plant employment would be partly off-set by decreases in the farm income of such operators. On the other hand, on farms where an increase in the value of farm output was reported as a result of operator employment at one of the new plants, one may expect that the effects of operator plant employment on non-farm income and on farm income would tend to reinforce one another, thus giving a greater effect on the total income of such operators than that which might be expected in cases where the effects on non-farm and farm income partly off-set one another.

In this connection it is therefore of interest to note that farm operators in the Tubbercurry area who reported that the value of their farm output had been increased as a result of plant employment reported that plant employment had led to a mean increase of £380 in annual household income. Those who reported that the value of farm output had been unaffected by plant employment reported a mean increase of £337 in annual household income, while those operators who said that the value of their farm output had decreased as a result of plant employment reported a mean increase of £317 in annual household income.

Similar income effects were reported in the Scarriff area. Farm operators who said that the value of their farm output had increased as a result of plant employment reported a mean increase of £329 in annual household income. Those who had indicated that plant employment had no effect on the value of their farm output reported that plant employment had led to a mean increase of £247 in annual household income. Farm operators who said that the value of their farm output had decreased as a result of their plant employment reported a mean increase of £197 in household income.

Thus, in each area greater increases in annual household incomes were reported by farm operators whose plant employment had resulted in increased farm output than by operators whose plant employment had not affected the value of their farm output. Increases in household incomes of the latter group were, in turn, greater than increases in household income reported by farm operators whose plant employment had led to a reduction in the value of their farm output.

13

Selectivity Factors

This chapter contains an examination of some selectivity factors which were expected to be of importance in the recruitment of employees of the new plants. Comparisons in respect of four groups are presented. In section A, personal and farm business characteristics of farm operators employed at the plant are compared with those of farm operators not employed at the plant in each area. Section B contains comparisons of personal data between non-heads of farm households employed at the plants and non-heads of farm households in the working age group who were not employed in the plants. Sections C and D incorporate similar comparisons for corresponding groups of heads of urban households and non-heads of urban households respectively.

A.   FARM OPERATORS

This section contains a discussion of the selectivity factors which differentiated farm operators who obtained plant employment from other farm operators in the two areas who were not employed at the new plants. The discussion is confined to the farm operators in each area who did not change their farm work association subsequent to obtaining employment at the new plants.

1. Personal characteristics

Certain personal characteristics of farm operators employed at the new plants were compared with the same characteristics of

182

a sample of farm operators in each of the two areas who had not been employed at the new plants.

As shown in table 72, the mean age of farm operators employed in Tubbercurry was 41.00 years, while the mean age of other

TABLE 72. Comparison of personal characteristics of farm operator plant employees and of other farm operators in each area

Characteristic	Tubbercurry		Scarriff	
	Plant employees	Other operators	Plant employees	Other operators
Mean age (years)	41.00**	52.97**	36.88**	51.33**
Mean post-primary education (years)	1.47	0.22	0.29	0.19
Per cent having post-primary education	46.66**	5.00**	17.65	5.06
Mean household size	3.80	3.04	3.82	3.96

** Difference significant at 99 per cent level.

farm operators in the area was 52.97 years. The difference had a high statistical significance. The mean age of farm operators employed at the Scarriff plant was 36.88 years while that of other farm operators in the Scarriff area was 51.33 years, the difference being highly significant statistically. Thus, farm operators in both areas who were employed at the plants tended to be younger than farm operators who were not employed, the mean difference observed being about 12 years in Tubbercurry and about $14\frac{1}{2}$ years in Scarriff.

In each of the two areas, the proportion of farm operators not employed at the plant who had obtained some formal post-primary education was about 5 per cent.[1] In contrast, the proportion of plant employee farm operators who had obtained some formal post-primary education was 46.6 per cent in Tubbercurry and 17.6 per cent in Scarriff. The difference observed in Tubber-

[1] This figure coincides with an estimate that 5 per cent of farmers in the West of Ireland in 1963 had obtained some full-time post-primary education. This estimate was prepared by Mr P. Keenan of the Irish Department of Agriculture and Fisheries (26).

curry was significant at the 99 per cent level, while the difference observed in Scarriff was not significant at the 95 per cent level.

This evidence indicates that there was selectivity among farm operators in the Tubbercurry area in regard to whether or not they had obtained any formal post-primary education. Such selectivity may have been mainly due to the hiring policies of the plant, since the general level of skills required by employees in Tubbercurry was higher than that in Scarriff. Hence, the hiring policies in Tubbercurry may have tended to select out for employment those people having some post-primary education more frequently than those having primary education only.

Farm operators employed in Tubbercurry had 1.25 years more post-primary education than those farm operators who were not employed. This difference was not quite significant at the 95 per cent level, but was significant at the 90 per cent level. It would thus appear that whether or not farm operators had had some post-primary education was relatively more important from a selectivity point of view than the actual amount of post-primary education obtained. Although farm operators employed in Scarriff had more post-primary education than those not employed, the difference was not statistically significant.

Differences in household size between farm operators with and without plant employment in both areas were not statistically significant.

2. Farm business characteristics

Data regarding land utilization and livestock numbers on farms operated by plant employees and other farm operators are shown in table 73. Direct effects of plant employment on land utilization and livestock numbers on farms operated by plant employees have been subtracted out from the actual values occurring on those farms, in order to estimate the degree of selectivity involved. For example, the mean number of acres farmed by the plant employees in Tubbercurry in 1966 was 30.06 acres. The mean direct effect of plant employment on the acreage farmed by these operators was an increase of 0.93 acres. Subtraction of this latter

TABLE 73. Comparison of land utilization and livestock numbers on farms operated by plant employees and on farms operated by other operators (allowing for the direct effects of plant employment on plant employees' farms)

Characteristic (mean)	Tubbercurry		Scarriff	
	Plant employees	Other operators	Plant employees	Other operators
Acres farmed	29.13**	43.50**	31.94**	60.76**
Acres of grain crops	2.06**	0.74**	1.58*	0.75*
Acres of root and green crops	1.37*	0.62*	1.98	1.15
Number of cows	4.00	4.64	4.82**	7.41**
Total number of cattle	15.60	17.60	17.53**	31.37**
Number of pigs	2.46	1.33	3.20	2.80
Number of poultry	33.33	24.00	22.82	22.48
Number of sheep	2.60	1.53	4.96	5.67

** Difference significant at the 99 per cent level.
* Difference significant at the 95 per cent level.

figure from the actual acreage reported yields the figure of 29.13 shown in table 73. Thus differences between the values shown in table 73 for attributes of plant employee farms and of other farms would reflect original differences between the two groups of farms, from which the incidence of selectivity may be estimated.

Highly significant differences appeared in both areas in the number of acres farmed. Farm operators who had obtained plant employment had come from smaller farms. This was as expected on a priori grounds. Since a desire for increased income is usually an important motivating force in prompting a decision to seek a non-farm job, it may be expected that farm operators having lower farm incomes would have offered their labour services more frequently to the new plants than would have farm operators with larger incomes. To the extent that farm income is related to the number of acres farmed, one would expect that offers of labour services to industry would come more frequently from farm operators who were farming smaller acreages.

After allowing for the direct effects on grain crop acreage and on acreage of root and green crops on the farms operated by plant employees, significant differences in acreages devoted to these crops on the two groups of farms were found. In each area, the farm operators who obtained plant employment had had higher acreages under grain crops and under root and green crops than had farm operators who did not obtain plant employment. This suggests that those operators had been operating their farms more intensively in terms of cropping pattern in an effort to minimize income differences which might be expected to occur as a result of their lower farm size.

Numbers of cows and of all cattle had been significantly lower on farms operated by plant employees than on other farms in the Scarriff area. Numbers of these animals had also been lower on the farms of operators employed in Tubbercurry, but not significantly so. These data suggest, therefore, that farms whose operators obtained employment at the new plants in both areas had been smaller and had had a relatively greater emphasis placed on crop production than on cattle. It is of interest to note that the number of pigs on farms whose operators obtained plant employment had been somewhat higher in each area than on farms whose operators did not obtain plant employment, thus providing further evidence that farms from which operators had obtained plant employment had been operated relatively more intensively than other farms in the two areas.

The 1965–66 labour utilization and farm income data for farms whose operators had plant employment and for other farms in each area is shown in table 74. In both areas, as might be expected, the farm labour input of plant employee farm operators was substantially less than that of other farm operators.

In all labour, machinery value and farm income characteristics, the differences observed in 1966 between farms whose operators had obtained plant employment and farms operated by people who did not obtain plant employment were much greater in the Scarriff area than in the Tubbercurry area. For example, total family labour input on plant employee farms was about half of that on other farms in Scarriff, while the differences in Tubbercurry were slight.

Sales of farm products tended to be less on farms operated by

TABLE 74. Labour utilization and farm income on farms operated by plant employees and on other farms in each area during 1965-66

Characteristic (mean)	Tubbercurry		Scarriff	
	Plant employees	Other operators	Plant employees	Other operators
Number of family members doing some farm work	2.4	2.0	2.2	2.4
Manhours of operator labour	930**	1,578**	922**	2,051**
Total manhours of family labour	2,288	2,342	1,853**	3,772**
Number of days hired labour used	33	30	16	21
Value of farm machinery and equipment (£)	57	113	43*	122*
Total sales of farm products (£)	358	428	541*	851*
Household consumption of farm products (£)	86	82	80	90
Gross farm output (£)	444	510	621*	941*
Non-labour farm expenses (£)	213	242	310	302
Family and labour income (£)	231	268	311*	639*
Net family farm income (£)	190	240	295*	496*

** Difference significant at the 99 per cent level.
* Difference significant at the 95 per cent level.

plant employees than on other farms in each area, the difference being greater in Scarriff. As there were little differences in household consumption, gross farm output was also lower on farms operated by plant employees. Differences in non-labour farm expenses on plant employee farms and on other farms were slight in each area, so that family and labour income was lower on plant employee farms than on other farms.

The difference in farm income was much more pronounced in Scarriff than in Tubbercurry. In Scarriff, plant employee farms had a mean family and labour income of £311, compared to £639 on other farms, a difference of £328 which was significant at the 95 per cent level. In Tubbercurry, plant employee farms had a mean family and labour income of £231, which was £37 less than the mean family and labour income on farms whose operators did not obtain plant employment.

The data presented in table 74 are the actual data pertaining to the different groups of farms for the year immediately prior to the study being conducted. As such, the data pertaining to plant employee farms reflect the combined influence of the selectivity factors and of the direct industrialization effects on these farms arising from the employment of the operators of those farms at the new plants.

Evidence presented in the previous chapter suggests that substitution effects following plant employment of farm operators occurred more frequently on Tubbercurry farms than on Scarriff farms. The data in table 74 support this viewpoint. It will be observed that the mean number of family members doing some farm work on farms operated by plant employees in Tubbercurry was slightly higher than the mean number doing some farm work on other farms in the area. Such was not the case in Scarriff. As noted, the mean number of man-hours of all family labour used was only slightly less on plant employee farms than on other farms in the Tubbercurry area, whereas a large difference was apparent in the Scarriff area. Thus, in Tubbercurry other family members provided a much greater share of the farm labour on plant employee farms than on other farms in the area, while in

Scarriff this was not so. Similarly, the number of days of labour hired on farms whose operators had plant employment was slightly greater than on other farms in the Tubbercurry area. Once again, the reverse was true in Scarriff.

These greater substitutions on Tubbercurry farms for the loss of farm operator labour would lessen any differences which might exist between incomes on farms operated by plant employees and on other farms in the Tubbercurry area. While the farm output and income differences observed in Tubbercurry are not statistically significant at the 95 per cent level, it may be claimed that this was largely a result of the relatively small number of farm operators employed at the plant. Since only 15 operators were employed at the plant, mean differences between a sample of this size and the population of farm operators would need to be quite large before statistical significance at the 95 per cent level would occur.

All of the farm output and farm income differences between plant employee farms and other farms in the Tubbercurry area, though relatively small in magnitude, are in the direction expected on a priori grounds. It was expected that farm operators who obtained plant employment would tend to have smaller farm output and farm income levels than those not obtaining plant employment, since it was expected that operators of lower income farms would offer their labour services to industry more frequently than would other farm operators.

Since all of the observed farm output and farm income differences between farm operator plant employees and other farm operators in the Tubbercurry area were in the expected direction, it may well be that real differences existed between the two groups of farm operators in the area. However, because of the small sample size it is not possible to conclude at the 95 per cent level that the data regarding these observed differences confirm the existence of real differences in farm output and farm income characteristics between farm operators employed at the Tubbercurry plant and farm operators not employed at the Tubbercurry plant.

The obviously high magnitude of the substitution effects on the Tubbercurry farms would tend to narrow the farm income differences. It will also be recollected that a majority of farm operators who obtained plant employment in both areas reported that the value of farm output had increased or at least remained unchanged as a direct result of plant employment (through the substitution effects and the farm investment effects from increased household income). Hence, original differences in farm output and farm income between plant employee farms and other farms would be likely to be greater than the differences observed in table 74.

Finally, as the number of farm operators employed at the new plants who did not subsequently changed their farm work association was 15 in Tubbercurry and 17 in Scarriff, relatively large differences in farm characteristics would need to be observed before high statistical significance in mean differences would be achieved.

The evidence presented in this section, though stronger in the case of Scarriff than of Tubbercurry, suggests that farm operators who obtained plant employment were more likely to be younger than those who did not obtain plant employment, were more likely to have had some post-primary education, and were more likely to come from smaller, though more intensively operated farms, having lower farm sales, farm output, farm income and value of machinery and equipment than on farms whose operators did not obtain plant employment.

B.   NON-HEADS OF FARM HOUSEHOLDS

Certain personal characteristics of non-heads of farm households (apart from operators) who were employed at the new plants were compared with the same characteristics of non-heads of farm households who were not employed. The comparison was made against the characteristics of those non-heads of other farm households who belonged to the age group from 14 to 64 years inclusive.

The mean age of the non-heads of farm households employed at the Tubbercurry plant was 20.5 years, while the mean age of non-heads of farm households who were not employed at the plant and who were in the working age group was 33.9 years. This difference was found to be significant at the 99 per cent level.

Similarly, the mean age of employed non-heads of farm households in Scarriff was 26.4 years, compared with a mean age of 35.5 years for those not employed at the plant, the difference being significant at the 95 per cent level.

In Tubbercurry, the proportion of employee non-heads of farm households who had obtained some post-primary education was 69 per cent, compared with 35 per cent among those who did not obtain plant employment. The difference was significant at the 99 per cent level.

Similarly, the employed non-heads of farm households in Tubbercurry had a mean of 2.25 years of post-primary education, as opposed to a mean of 0.92 years for the group not employed at the plant. This difference was also significant at the 99 per cent level.

In Scarriff, on the other hand, the proportion of employed non-heads who had received some post-primary education (49 per cent) exceeded the proportion among those not employed at the plant (32 per cent). Similarly, the mean number of years of post-primary education obtained by employed non-heads of farm households (1.24 years) exceeded that obtained by those not employed (0.92 years). However, these differences were not significant at the 95 per cent level.

This evidence suggests that in both areas there was a high degree of selectivity based on age involved in the obtaining of plant employment by non-heads of farm households. Post-primary education was also important in Tubbercurry in this regard, but not as important in Scarriff.

C. HEADS OF URBAN HOUSEHOLDS

From data collected in the survey of the heads of urban households which contained no plant employees, personal characteristics of those heads were extracted for comparison with the same characteristics of heads of urban households who had obtained plant employment.

Once again, as shown in table 75, a strong selectivity based on age was apparent. This was significant at the 99 per cent level

TABLE 75. Comparison of personal characteristics of heads of urban households employed at the new plants and heads of urban households containing no plant employees

Characteristic	Tubbercurry		Scarriff	
	Plant employees	Other heads	Plant employees	Other heads
Mean age (years)	33.38**	54.26**	40.86**	55.05**
Mean post-primary education (years)	1.96	1.63	1.00	1.39
Per cent having post-primary education	73.07**	40.27**	32.00	33.76
Mean household size	2.84	3.38	4.10*	3.13*

** Difference significant at the 99 per cent level.
* Difference significant at the 95 per cent level.

in each area. In Tubbercurry, whether or not heads of urban households had obtained post-primary education was a highly significant factor though it appeared that this was, as in the case of farm operators, more important than the actual amount of post-primary education received.

Post-primary education was not a factor involved in selectivity affecting the plant employment of heads of urban households in Scarriff. However, the difference in size of household between those heads of urban households employed at the plant and those heads of households which contained no plant employees was significant at the 95 per cent level. Other things being equal, heads of households containing more numbers would be expected to have a greater incentive to seek plant employment than would heads of smaller households, because of greater requirements of income. However, such a selectivity factor could be easily outweighed by other selectivity factors, especially those involving the hiring policies of the new firm. It is therefore of interest to note that in the case of heads of urban households in the Scarriff area, among whom only slight post-primary educational differences were noted, a significant selectivity based on household size was evident.

D.   NON-HEADS OF URBAN HOUSEHOLDS

Characteristics of non-heads of urban households who obtained plant employment were compared with those of non-heads of urban households containing no plant employees. Only those non-heads of urban households in the 14–64 year working-age group were considered in making the comparison.

Once again, a highly significant selectivity based on age was apparent. Urban non-heads employed at the Tubbercurry plant had a mean age of 22.08 years; those not employed at the plant had a mean age of 30.30 years. In Scarriff, the corresponding figures were 22.0 years and 33.05 years respectively. The difference in each case was significant at the 99 per cent level.

The comparison of non-heads of urban households based on education was quite interesting. The mean number of years of post-primary education obtained by non-heads of urban households who were not employed at the plant was higher than that obtained by those who were employed.

Non-heads of urban households who were not employed at the plant had a mean of 3.25 years of post-primary education while those employed at the plant had a mean of 2.16 years. The difference was significant at the 95 per cent level. The corresponding figures for non-heads of urban households in the Scarriff area were 2.16 and 1.76 years respectively.

These data indicate that, especially in Tubbercurry, the selectivity factors based on education tended to favour the employment of persons having about 2 years of post-primary education. It is of interest to note that this is the length of the basic vocational school course, while the secondary school course of study is of longer duration. This selectivity on the basis of post-primary education is as might be expected on an a priori basis, since plant managers would be more likely to have hiring policies which favour the employment of those having vocational school as opposed to non-technical secondary school training.

14

Summary and Conclusions

In an attempt to generate additional employment opportunities in Western Ireland, the Irish government has assisted the establishment of many new manufacturing plants in predominantly rural areas. The present study was designed to investigate the impact of such industrialization on two areas in Western Ireland, one around Tubbercurry, Co. Sligo and the other around Scarriff, Co. Clare, in both of which medium-sized industrial plants had been located.

Hypotheses were developed regarding the likely effect of the new industrial plants on employment, population, incomes and expenditure in the two areas. In general, it was found that the plants had had a substantial direct employment effect on the two areas. It was estimated that the plants had directly increased employment in the Tubbercurry area by 133 persons and in the Scarriff area by 134 persons, relative to the level of employment which would have obtained in these areas in the absence of the new plants. About three fourths of these Tubbercurry employees and about half of the Scarriff employees would, in the absence of the new plants, have gone to places outside Ireland in search of employment. Nearly all of the employment effects occurred within a radius of 12 miles of the new plants.

The direct population effect on the two areas was estimated as an increase of 231 in the Tubbercurry area and an increase of 318 in the Scarriff area relative to what the population would have been in the two areas in the absence of the two plants. The

195

employment and population effects were greater in and close to the towns in which the new plants were located.

About three fourths of the plant employees reported that an increase in their household incomes had occurred as a result of their obtaining employment at the new plants. Some people had returned from abroad in order to take employment at the new plants. Most of these people had experienced a reduction in household income.

Part of the increased household income was placed in savings accounts, but most of it was spent. However, not all was spent within the areas. Many respondents reported spending the major part of their increased income in towns outside the areas. These leakages would tend to reduce the indirect effects of industrialization which would be generated by a multiplier effect on employment and incomes in the two areas. Within the two areas, there was some shift in shopping from outlying towns to the towns in which the plants were located. Such shopping shifts tended to feature such items as groceries more frequently than durable items.

Many farm residents obtained employment at the new plants. However, relatively few of these, 15 in Tubbercurry and 17 in Scarriff, were farm operators. In the majority of cases, employment of farm operators at the new plants did not lead to a reduction in their farm output. In fact, in many instances farm operators reported an increase in farm output as a result of their plant employment.

Considerable labour substitution occurred on farms whose operators had taken plant employment. Often, the operator gave up some former leisure time in order to do farm work. Rising earlier and working into evening time were reported in many instances. Farmers' wives and other family members usually did more farm work than formerly on these farms, so that in many cases total amount of time spent by all the farm family at farm work did not decrease.

Increased use was also made of the farmers' own machinery and equipment and hired machinery and equipment tended to be used more frequently as a result of the operator obtaining plant employment.

In addition to these substitution effects, there were also strong farm investment effects from the increased household income obtained by farm operators who obtained plant employment. Some of these operators bought or rented extra land. Most operators bought additional livestock. Investment in fertilizers was frequently mentioned. As a result of these substitution and investment effects, plant employment of farm operators did not, in general, result in reductions in farm output.

In general, in both areas, plant employment of farm operators led to a shift from labour-intensive to labour-extensive enterprises on their farms. Decreases occurred in acreage of grain, root and green crops and corresponding increases occurred in the acreage under grassland. In general, also, there was a reduction in numbers of pigs and an increase in the number of dry cattle kept.

Evidence obtained during the study indicates that there were important selectivity factors at work in both areas which led to differences being apparent between those area residents who obtained plant employment and those who did not. Farm operators who obtained plant employment tended to come from smaller than average farms in each area, having smaller than average inventories of farm machinery and equipment. Their farms, however, tended to have been operated somewhat more intensively, in terms of cropping pattern, than other farms in the two areas. Farm output and farm income tended to have been lower on these farms than on others in the areas. Such farm operators would have had greater incentive to seek plant employment in order to obtain extra income.

Selectivity was also associated with personal characteristics. Farm operators employed at the plants were more likely to be younger than average and were more likely to have had some post-primary education. These selectivity factors applied not only to farm operators but also to non-heads of farm households, heads of urban households and non-heads of urban households. Within each of these groups, those people who obtained plant employment were more likely to be younger than those who did not. Selectivity regarding education was more pronounced in the Tubbercurry area, where the general level of skills required at the plant was higher than in the case of the Scarriff plant.

This study demonstrated that in the two areas, industrialization had led to increases in employment, population and incomes. Industrialization had also led to the acceptance of non-farm employment by some farm people. When farm operators were employed, reductions in their farm output were not usually necessitated as a result of their plant employment. These effects, arising from the location of medium sized industrial plants in small towns, tended to pervade through an area having a radius of about 12 miles around the plants.

Further research deemed desirable would involve a comparison of the magnitude and spatial incidence of the direct effects of medium sized industrial establishments located in predominantly rural areas with the magnitude and spatial incidence of the direct effects of the location of larger industrial establishments in industrial estates, such as that at Shannon Airport.

Another avenue of exploration which would complement the present study would involve estimation of the indirect effects of industrialization on the two areas studied. Such indirect effects would arise from changes in the external environment in which firms and households function. The total impact of industrialization on these areas would include the direct effects estimated in the present study and the indirect effects which would result via a multiplier effect.

List of Works

1. Bellerby, J. R. *Agriculture and industry: relative income.* New York, N.Y., St Martin's Press. 1956.
2. Demas, William G. *The economics of development in small countries, with special reference to the Caribbean.* Montreal, Canada, McGill University Press. 1965.
3. Domar, Evsey D. *Essays in the theory of economic growth.* New York, N.Y., Oxford University Press. 1957.
4. Evans, Gordon, ed. *War on want.* New York, N.Y., The Macmillan Company. 1962.
5. Fei, John C. H., and Ranis, Gustav. *Development of the labor surplus economy: theory and policy.* Homewood, Ill., Richard D. Irwin, Inc. 1964.
6. Fennell, Rosemary. *Industrialisation and agricultural development in the congested districts.* An Foras Taluntais Economic Research Series No. 2. 1962.
7. Freeman, T. W. *Ireland.* New York, N.Y., E. P. Dutton, Inc. 1950.
8. Harrod, Roy F. *Towards a dynamic economics.* London, England, The Macmillan Company. 1948.
9. Heady, Earl O. "Research and economic development: needs, opportunities and problems." In Haroldsen, Edwin, ed. *Food: one tool in international development.* Ames, Iowa, Iowa State University Press. 1963.
10. ———— and Tweeten, Luther G. *Resource demand and structure in the agricultural industry.* Ames, Iowa, Iowa State University Press. 1963.
11. Healy, John. *Death of an Irish town.* Cork, Ireland, Mercier Press. 1968.

12. Hirschman, Albert O. *The strategy of economic development*. New Haven, Conn., Yale University Press. 1958.

13. *Ireland. An Foras Tionscal. Statutory report and accounts for the year ended 31st March, 1956.* 1956.

14. ———. *Statutory report and accounts for the year ended 31st March, 1960.* 1960.

15. ———. *Statutory report and accounts for the year ended 31st March, 1961.* 1961.

16. ———. *Statutory report and accounts for the year ended 31st March, 1962.* 1962.

17. ———. *Statutory report and accounts for the year ended 31st March, 1963.* 1963.

18. ———. *Statutory report and accounts for the year ended 31st March, 1964.* 1964.

19. ———. *Statutory report and accounts for the year ended 31st March, 1965.* 1965.

20. ———. *Statutory report and accounts for the year ended 31st March, 1966.* 1966.

21. Ireland, Government of. *Budget, 1967*. Dublin, Ireland, Stationery Office. 1967.

22. *Ireland. Oireachtas na hEireann. Undeveloped Areas Act, 1952.* 1952.

23. ———. *Undeveloped Areas (Amendment) Act, 1957.* 1957.

24. ———. *Undeveloped Areas (Amendment) Act, 1963.* 1963.

25. Jorgensen, Dale W. "The development of a dual economy." *Economic Journal* 71:309–334. 1961.

26. Keenan, Patrick. *Personal communication to author*. 1969.

27. Keynes, John M. *The general theory of employment, interest and money*. New York, N.Y., Harcourt, Brace and Company. 1937.

28. Leibenstein, Harvey. *Economic backwardness and economic growth*. New York, N.Y., John Wiley and Sons, Inc. 1957.

29. Lewis, W. Arthur. *The principles of economic planning*. London, England, Denis Dobson, Limited. 1949.

30. Mandelbaum, Kurt. *The industrialisation of backward areas.* Oxford, England, Basil Blackwell. 1945.

31. Mountjoy, Alan B. *Industrialization and underdeveloped countries.* London, England, Hutchinson University Library. 1963.

32. Myrdal, Gunnar. *An international economy.* New York, N.Y., Harper and Brothers. 1956.

33. Nicholls, William H. " 'Agricultural surplus' as a factor in economic development." *Journal of Political Economy* 71:1–29. 1963.

34. Olson, Manchur. "Agriculture and the depressed areas." *Journal of Farm Economics* 46:984–988. 1964.

35. Rosenstein-Rodan, P. N. "Problems of industrialisation of eastern and south-eastern Europe." *Economic Journal* 53:202–211. 1943.

36. Schultz, Theodore W. *Transforming traditional agriculture.* New Haven, Conn., Yale University Press. 1964.

37. Smith, Eldon D. "Restrictions on policy alternatives relating to underdeveloped regions of developed countries." *Journal of Farm Economics* 48:1227–1231. 1966.

38. Staley, Eugene and Morse, Richard, *Modern small industry for developing countries.* New York, N.Y., McGraw-Hill Book Company. 1965.

39. Wharton, Clifton R. "Modernizing subsistence agriculture." In Weiner, Myron, ed. *Modernization: the dynamics of growth.* Pp. 258–269. New York, N.Y., Basic Books, Inc. 1966.

40. Young, Arthur. *A tour in Ireland with general observations on the present state of that kingdom.* London, England, T. Cadell and J. Dodsley. 1780.

Appendix A

This appendix contains a listing of the Rural Districts and District Electoral Divisions included in the study areas.

A. THE TUBBERCURRY AREA

The Tubbercurry area comprised the Rural District of Tubbercurry, Co. Sligo, together with the District Electoral Divisions of Kilfree, Kilshalvey No. 1 and Kilshalvey No. 2 in Boyle No. 2 Rural District, Co. Sligo, the District Electoral Divisions of Ballymote and Carrickbanagher in Sligo Rural District, Co. Sligo, and the District Electoral Divisions of Cloonmore, Doocastle, Kilbeagh, Sonnagh and Tungesh in Swinford Rural District, Co. Mayo.

B. THE SCARRIFF AREA

The Scarriff area comprised the Rural District of Scarriff, Co. Clare, together with the District Electoral Divisions of Fahymore, Killokennedy, Kilseily and Lackareagh in Meelick Rural District, Co. Clare, and the District Electoral Divisions of Ballinahinch, Glandree, Killaneena, Killuran and Loughea in Tulla Rural District, Co. Clare.

Index

203

Index by Brenda Hall
Registered indexer of the Society
of Indexers